POPULATION GEOGRAPHY

POPULATION GEOGRAPHY

Hemant Kumar Doniwal

GNOSIS

Publishers of Educational Books

Worldwide Circulation through Authorspress Global Network
First Published 2008
by
GNOSIS
E-35/103, Jawahar Park
Laxmi Nagar, Delhi-110 092
e-mail: authorspress@yahoo.com

An Imprint of Authorspress

Population Geography
ISBN 81-89012-52-5

Printed in India at Virgo Press, Delhi.

Preface

An important subdivision of human geography, population geography is one of the most recent fields in geographical research and one which holds extreme relevance in the context of today's world. Population geography is a field which concerns itself with the spatial variations in the distributed composition, migration and growth of populations, and their relations to the nature of places. Involving demography in a spatial context, population geography attempts at delineating mankinds's relation to the environment and spatial patterns of the earth, through the prism of demographic studies.

Population geography is a crucial emerging subject, which brings within its purview such issues as the study of people in their spatial distribution and density, increase or decrease in population numbers, movement and mobility of population occupational structures, grouping of people in settlements, geographical character of places, ways in which places react to population phenomena, et. The book explores all these issues which circumscribe population geography, its relevance and contributions, and its future. It also delves into current trends and developments, making the book more upto-date with statistics and diagrams furthering this feature.

The book has been written in a lucid style and is illustrated with diagrams and tables for right interpretation of geographical facts. The book will be of immense help for undergraduate and postgraduate students of geography in particular and the students of demography, sociology and economics in general. It will also be useful to engineers, academicians, scholars and general readers who are interested in population problems.

Hemant Kumar Doniwal

Contents

1
Introduction

Population geography is the study of the ways in which spatial variations in the distribution, composition, migration, and growth of populations are related to the nature of places. Population geography involves demography in a geographical perspective. It focuses on the characteristics of population distributions that change in a spatial context. Examples can be shown through population density maps. A few types of maps that show the spatial layout of population are chloropleth, isoline, and dot maps. Demography studies:

- Study of people in their spatial distribution and density
- Increase or decrease in population numbers
- The movements and mobility of populations
- Occupational Structure
- Grouping of people in settlements
- The way from the geographical character of places e.g. settlement patterns
- The way in which places in turn react to population phenomena e.g. immigration.

1.1. Demography

Demography is the statistical study of all populations. It can be a general science that can be applied to any kind of dynamic population, that is, one that changes over time or space. It encompasses the study of the size, structure and distribution of populations, and spatial and/or temporal changes in them in response to birth, death, migration and aging.

Demographic analysis can be applied to whole societies or to groups defined by criteria such as education, nationality, religion and ethnicity. In academia, demography is often regarded as a branch of either economics or sociology. Formal demography limits its object of study to the measurement of populations processes, while the more broad field of social demography population studies also analyse the relationships between economic, social, cultural and biological processes influencing a population.

The term demographics is often used erroneously for demography, but refers rather to selected population characteristics as used in government, marketing or opinion research, or the demographic profiles used in such research.

1.2. Methods of Data Collection

There are two methods of data collection: direct and indirect. Direct data come from vital statistics registries that track all births and deaths as well as certain changes in legal status such as marriage, divorce, and migration (registration of place of residence). In developed countries with good registration systems (such as the United States and much of Europe), registry statistics are the best method for estimating the number of births and deaths.

The census is the other common direct method of collecting demographic data. A census is usually conducted by a national government and attempts to enumerate every person in a country. However, in contrast to vital statistics data, which are typically collected continuously and summarised on an annual basis, censuses typically occur only every 10 years or so, and thus are not usually the best source of data on births and deaths. Analyses are conducted after a census to estimate how much over or undercounting took place. Censuses do more than just count people. They also typically collect information about families or households, as well as about such individual characteristics as age, sex, marital status, literacy/education, employment status and occupation, and geographical location. They may also collect data on migration (or place of birth or of previous residence), language, religion, nationality (or ethnicity or race), and citizenship. In countries in which the vital registration system may be incomplete, the censuses are also used as a direct source of information about fertility and mortality; for example the censuses of the People's Republic of China gather information on births and deaths that occurred in the 18 months immediately preceding the census.

Indirect methods of data collections are required in countries where full data are not available, such as is the case in much of the developing world. One of these techniques is the sister method, where survey researchers ask women how many of their sisters have died or had children and at what age. With these surveys, researchers can then indirectly estimate birth or death rates for the entire population. Other indirect methods include asking people about siblings, parents, and children.

There are a variety of demographic methods for modeling population processes. They include models of mortality, fertility, marriage, disability, population projections, and population momentum.

Important concepts in demography include-:

— The crude birth rate, the annual number of live births per thousand people.

— The general fertility rate, the annual number of live births per 1000 women of childbearing age (often taken to be from 15 to 49 years old, but sometimes from 15 to 44).

— Age-specific fertility rates, the annual number of live births per 1000 women in particular age groups (usually age 15-19, 20-24 etc.)

— The crude death rate, the annual number of deaths per 1000 people.

— The infant mortality rate, the annual number of deaths of children less than 1 year old per 1000 live births.

— The expectation of life (or life expectancy), the number of years which an individual at a given age could expect to live at present mortality levels.

— The total fertility rate, the number of live births per woman completing her reproductive life, if her childbearing at each age reflected current age-specific fertility rates.

— The gross reproduction rate, the number of daughters who would be born to a woman completing her reproductive life at current age-specific fertility rates.

— The net reproduction ratio is the expected number of daughters, per newborn prospective mother, who may or may not survive to and through the ages of childbearing.

Note that the crude death rate as defined above and applied to a whole population can give a misleading impression. For example, the number of deaths per 1000 people can be higher for developed nations than in less-developed countries, despite standards of health being better in developed countries. This is because developed countries have relatively more older people, who are more likely to die in a given year, so that the overall mortality rate can be higher even if the mortality rate at any given age is lower. A more complete picture of mortality is given by a life table which summarises mortality separately at each age. A life table is necessary to give a good estimate of life expectancy.

The fertility rates can also give a misleading impression that a population is growing faster than it in fact is, because measurement of fertility rates only involves the reproductive rate of women, and does not adjust for the sex ratio. For example, if a population has a total fertility rate of 4.0 but the sex ratio is 66/34 (twice as many men as women), this population is actually growing at a slower natural increase rate than would a population having a fertility rate of 3.0 and a sex ratio of 50/50. This distortion is greatest in India and Myanmar, and is present in China as well.

Ibn Khaldun (1332-1406) is regarded as the "father of demography" for his economic analysis of social organisation which produced the first scientific and theoretical work on population, development, and group dynamics.

At the end of the 18th century, Thomas Malthus concluded that, if unchecked, populations would be subject to exponential growth. He feared that population growth would tend to outstrip growth in food production, leading to ever increasing famine and poverty; he is seen as the intellectual father of ideas of overpopulation and the limits to growth. Later more sophisticated and realistic models were presented by e.g. Benjamin Gompertz and Verhulst.

1.3. Demographic Transition

Contrary to Malthus' predictions (though in line with his thoughts on moral restraint), natural population growth in most developed countries has diminished to close to zero, without being held in check by famine or lack of resources, as people in developed nations have shown a tendency to have fewer children. The fall in population growth has occurred despite large rises in life expectancy in these countries. This pattern of population growth, with slow (or no) growth in post-industrial societies, followed by fast growth as the society develops and industrialises, followed by slow growth again as it becomes more affluent, is known as the demographic transition.

Similar trends are now becoming visible in ever more developing countries, so that far from spiralling out of control, world population growth is expected to slow markedly in the next century, coming to an eventual standstill or even declining. The change is likely to be accompanied by major shifts in the proportion of world population in particular regions. The United Nations Population Division expects the absolute number of infants and toddlers in the world to begin to fall by 2015, and the number of children under 15 by 2025.

The UN "medium" projection shows world population reaching an approximate equilibrium at 9 billion by 2075. Working independently, demographers at the International Institute for Applied Systems Analysis in Austria expect world population to peak at 9 billion by 2070. Throughout the 21st century, the average age of the population is likely to continue to rise.

1.4. Science of Population

Populations change through three processes: fertility, mortality, and migration. Fertility involves the number of children that women have and is to be contrasted with fecundity (a woman's childbearing potential). Mortality is the study of the causes, consequences, and measurement of processes affecting death to members of the population. Demographers most commonly study mortality using the Life Table, a statistical device which provides information about the mortality conditions (most notably the life expectancy) in the population. Migration refers to the movement of persons from an origin place to a destination place across some pre-defined, political boundary.

Migration researchers do not designate movements 'migrations' unless they are somewhat permanent. Thus demographers do not consider tourists and travelers to be migrating. While demographers who study migration typically do so through census data on place of residence, indirect sources of data including tax forms and labor force surveys are also important. Demography is today widely taught in many universities across the world, attracting students with initial training in social sciences, statistics or health.

Being at the crossroads of several disciplines such as geography, economics, sociology or epidemiology, demography offers tools to approach a large range of population issues by combining a more technical quantitative approach that represents the core of the discipline with many other methods borrowed from social or other sciences. Demographic research is conducted in universities, in research institutes as well as in statistical departments and in several international agencies.

References

John Bongaarts, "The Fertility-Inhibiting Effects of the Intermediate Fertility Variables", *Studies in Family Planning,* Vol. 13, No. 6/7. Jun. - Jul., 1982.

Longman, Phillip, *The Empty Cradle: how falling birth rates threaten global prosperity and what to do about it,* 2004.

McFalls, Joe, *Population: A Lively Introduction,* Population Reference Bureau, 2007

Preston, Samuel, Patrick Heuveline, and Michel Guillot, *Demography: Measuring and Modeling Population Processes,* Blackwell Publishing, 2000.

Wattenberg, Ben J., *How the New Demography of Depopulation Will Shape Our Future,* Chicago: R. Dee, 2004.

2
Demographic Transition

2.1. Introduction

Before the start of the demographic transition, life was short, births were many, growth was slow and the population was young. During the transition, first mortality and then fertility declined, causing population growth rates first to accelerate and then to slow again, moving toward low fertility, long life and an old population. The transition began around 1800 with declining mortality in Europe. It has now spread to all parts of the world and is projected to be completed by 2100. This global demographic transition has brought momentous changes, reshaping the economic and demographic life cycles of individuals and restructuring populations. Since 1800, global population size has already increased by a factor of six and by 2100 will have risen by a factor of ten. There will then be 50 times as many elderly, but only five times as many children; thus, the ratio of elders to children will have risen by a factor of ten. The length of life, which has already more than doubled, will have tripled, while births per woman will have dropped from six to two. In 1800, women spent about 70 percent of their adult years bearing and rearing young children, but that fraction has decreased in many parts of the world to only about 14 percent, due to lower fertility and longer life.

2.2. Demographic Transition

Demographic transition occurs in societies that transition from high birth rates and high death rates to low birth rates and low death rates as part of the economic development of a country from a pre-industrial to an industrialised economy. Usually it is described through the "Demographic Transition Model" (DTM) that describes the population changes over time. It is based on an interpretation begun in 1929 by the American demographer Warren Thompson of prior observed changes, or transitions, in birth and death rates in industrialised societies over the past two hundred years. Most developed countries are already in stage four of the model, the majority of developing countries are in stage 2 or stage 3, and no country is currently still in stage 1. The model has explained human population evolution relatively well in Europe and other highly developed countries. Many developing countries have moved into stage 3. The major exceptions are poor countries, mainly in sub-Saharan Africa and several Middle Eastern countries, which are poor or affected by government policy or civil strife, notably Pakistan, Palestine, Yemen and Afghanistan.

2.2.1. Stage One

In pre-industrial society death rates and birth rates were both high and fluctuated rapidly according to natural events, such as drought and disease, to produce a relatively constant and young population. Children contributed to the economy of the household from an early age by carrying water, firewood, and messages, caring for younger siblings, sweeping, washing dishes, preparing food, and doing some work in the fields. Raising a child cost little more than feeding him: there were no education or entertainment expenses, and in equatorial Africa, there were no clothing expenses either. Thus, the total cost of raising children barely exceeded their contribution to the household. In addition, as they became adults they became a major input into the family business, mainly farming, and were the primary form of insurance in old age. In India an adult son was all that prevented a widow from falling into destitution. While death rates remained high there was no question as to the need for children, even if the means to prevent them had existed.

2.2.2. Stage Two

This stage leads to a fall in death rates and an increase in population. The changes leading to this stage in Europe were initiated in the Agricultural Revolution of the 18th century and were initially quite slow. In the 20th century, the falls in death rates in developing countries tended to be substantially faster. Significant improvements in public health reduce mortality, particularly in childhood. These are not so much medical breakthroughs as they are improvements in water supply, growing scientific knowledge of the causes of disease and the improved education and social status of mothers.

A consequence of the decline in mortality in Stage Two is an increasingly rapid rise in population growth as the gap between deaths and births grows wider. Note that this growth is not due to an increase in fertility (or birth rates) but to a decline in deaths. This change in population occurred in northwestern Europe during the 19th century due to the Industrial Revolution. During the second half of the 20th century less-developed countries entered Stage Two, creating the worldwide population explosion that has demographers concerned today.

Another characteristic of Stage Two of the demographic transition is a change in the age structure of the population. In Stage One, the majority of deaths are concentrated in the first 5-10 years of life. Therefore, more than anything else, the decline in death rates in Stage Two entails the increasing survival of children and a growing population. Hence, the age structure of the population becomes increasingly youthful and more of these children enter the reproductive cycle of their lives while maintaining the high fertility rates of their parents. The bottom of the "age pyramid" widens first, accelerating population growth. The age structure of such a population is illustrated by using an example from the Third World today.

2.2.3. Stage Three

Stage Three moves the population towards stability through a decline in the birth rate. The resulting changes in the age structure of the population include a reduction in the youth dependency ratio and eventually population aging. The population structure becomes less triangular and more like an elongated balloon. During the period between the decline in youth dependency and rise in old age dependency there is a demographic window of opportunity that can potentially produce economic growth through an increase in the ratio of working age to dependent population; the demographic dividend. However, unless factors such as those listed above are allowed to work, a society's birth rates may not drop to a low level in due time, which means that the society cannot proceed to Stage Four and is locked in what is called a demographic trap.

2.2.4. Stage Four

Traditionally many demographers have assumed that the demographic transition would be complete when populations reached similarly low birth and death rates so that populations would become essentially stable, although no convincing social mechanism has been put forward for this view. The original Demographic Transition model has just four stages, but it is now widely accepted that a fifth stage is needed to represent countries that have undergone the economic transition from manufacturing based industries into service and information based industries called de-industrialisation. Countries such as Germany, Italy, Spain, Portugal, Greece and most notably Japan, whose populations are now reproducing well below their replacement levels, that is they are not producing enough children to replace their parent's generation. China, South Korea, Hong Kong, Singapore, Thailand and Cuba are also below replacement, but this is not producing a fall in population yet in these countries, because their populations are relatively young due to strong growth in the recent past. The population of southern Europe is already falling and Japan and some of western Europe will soon begin to fall without significant immigration. However, many countries that now have sub-replacement fertility did not reach this stage gradually but rather suddenly as a result of economic crisis brought on by the post-communist transition in the late 1980's and the 1990's. Examples include Russia, Ukraine, and the Baltic States. The population of these countries is falling due to fertility decline, emigration and, particularly in Russia, increased male mortality.

2.2.5. Criticisms of the DTM

2.2.5.1. Non-applicability to Less Developed Countries

One of the principal criticisms of the DTM is the questionable applicability to less developed countries, where the prerequisites for wealth and information access are limited. Applicability of the DTM to less developed countries has been questioned on several grounds. For example, the DTM has been validated primarily in Europe, Japan and North America where demographic data exists over centuries, whereas high quality demographic data for most LDCs did not become widely available until the mid 20th century. Secondly, the DTM does not account for recent phenomena such as AIDS; fully 94 percent of all HIV cases are found in underdeveloped countries, and thus the mortality decline of most of Sub-Saharan Africa has been arrested starting in the mid-1990s. This trend is so marked that two thirds of children in many sub-Saharan African countries are projected to have HIV infection by the time they have reached age 50 (or die from HIV before). In these areas HIV has become the leading source of mortality. Some trends in waterborne bacterial infant mortality are also disturbing in countries like Malawi, Sudan and Nigeria; for example, progress in the DTM model clearly arrested and reversed between 1975 and 2005. The above data lead to the questioning of the applicability to many lesser developed countries. DTM is used widely to minimise concerns regarding overpopulation and paint an overly optimistic version of the future.

2.2.5.2. Neo-Malthusian objections

The DTM is used to classify countries into general groups. Hence, it is unable to take into account evolutionary changes in the process of population growth and classify diverse population into distinct but coherent stages of the development process. Neo-Malthusians argue that the long-term fertility of a population depends on the most rapidly-breeding subgroups within the population. If a rapidly-breeding subgroup sustains its high fertility, it will eventually expand its numbers and restore the whole population to higher fertility.

All over the world groups with lower income, lower educational levels and more traditional social beliefs have higher fertility. In most countries poor parents decide to have many children and invest little in education, which implies that more weight gets placed on such families. Consequently, an increase in inequality lowers average education and, therefore, economic growth. Until now, DTM provides no explanation for this demographic-economic paradox and its possible dysgenic consequences, which may cause a cyclic behaviour of human population dynamics.

This is similar to the evolution of resistance to pesticides in insects, and to antibiotics among pathogens: the first applications kill large numbers, but a few surviving resistant individuals may eventually make good on the losses through exponential growth. In other words, a criticism of the DTM is that it is only valid if the fertility-lowering social changes that caused the DTM in present-day industrial nations permanently lower the fertility of every subgroup within each nation (which would imply no tendency of high-fertility individuals to produce high-fertility offspring). Garrett Hardin doubted that purely voluntary birth control could achieve that result; Hardin argued that voluntary birth control merely selects against the people who will use it.

This view appears to be an echo of the eugenics movement of the early 20th century, which was concerned that various minority groups would overwhelm the US or German populations in the long run through higher fertility and immigration. While "overwhelm" may be an excessively alarmist term, the white population in the United States certainly is declining in percentage terms in the 21st century. At the contrary, the critics of the Neo-Malthusian view believe that all human subgroups are subject to social and economic changes and that this is likely to overwhelm any tendency for a subgroup to have higher fertility in the long run. However, Hardin's doubts in the sufficiency of purely voluntary birth control were not based on group behaviour but on individual variation. Regardless of what the average fertility is for any group, some people will have more children than the mean for their group, and some will have fewer. According to Hardin, if the daughters of a woman who bore more children than the mean for her group go on to bear more children than the mean for their generation and group, this could be evidence for some sort of heritability of individual fertility, i.e., resistance to the cultural factors that lower the average fertility. If such resistance is heritable (whether culturally or genetically), then over time the percentage of people who are resistant could increase enough to create an entire population with a kind of "pesticide resistance" to the factors that gave rise to the demographic transition in the previously susceptible population, and population growth could resume. However, this effect would require several generations of sustained selection to become visible, if only a small percentage of people were initially carriers of this supposed resistance, and by then culture may have changed in other unpredictable ways.

2.2.5.3. *Generalisation from European experience*

The DTM is also limited in the sense that it gives a generalised picture of population change over time based on European studies, assuming that all countries would follow suit. In addition, the DTM is rigid in assuming that all countries will go through the stages 1 to 4 in that exact order. There are variables and exceptions such as war and turmoil that may lead to different results. Some countries may even skip stages. Demographic data for lesser developed countries span about five decades compared to 30 or more decades for developed countries, leading to questionable extrapolation of the experiences of the most developed countries.

2.3. Before the Demographic Transition

According to a famous essay by Thomas Malthus, first published in 1798, slow population growth was no accident. Population was held in equilibrium with the slowly growing economy. Faster population growth would depress wages, causing mortality to rise due to famine, war or disease-in short, misery. Malthus called this mortality response the "positive" check. Depressed wages would also cause postponement of marriage, resulting in prostitution and other vices, including contraception; this he called the "preventive" check. Since population could potentially grow more rapidly than the economy, it was always held in check by misery and vice, which were therefore the inevitable human lot. Economic progress could help only temporarily since population could soon grow to its new equilibrium level, where misery and vice would again hold it in check. Only through moral restraint-that is, the chaste postponement of marriage-did Malthus believe that humanity might avoid this fate, and he thought this an unlikely outcome. For pre-industrial Europe at least, Malthus seems to have been right. Population was held weakly in equilibrium by the positive and preventive checks. When weather, disease or political disturbance knocked population out of equilibrium, real wages and rents reacted strongly, and the checks brought population slowly back to equilibrium.

In western Europe in the centuries before 1800, marriage required the resources to establish and maintain a separate household, so age at first marriage for women was late, averaging around 25 years, and a substantial share of women never married. Although fertility was high within marriage, the total fertility rate (TFR) was moderate overall at four to five births per woman. Mortality was also moderately high, with life expectancy at birth between 25 and 35 years, but this was heavily influenced by high mortality in infancy and childhood. Population growth rates were generally low, averaging 0.3 percent/year before 1700 in western Europe, but sometimes rising above 1 percent in the nineteenth century. In Canada and the United States, marriage was much earlier because land was abundant, and population at first grew rapidly, but then decelerated in the nineteenth century.

Outside of Europe and its offshoots, fertility and mortality were higher in the pre-transitional period, and change in fertility and mortality came later. Data on mortality or fertility are only occasionally available for third-world countries before World War II. In India in the late nineteenth century, life expectancy averaged in the low 20s and was highly variable, while fertility was six or seven. The Total Fertility Rate is the sum across all ages of the birth rates at each age and, therefore, measures the total number of births a surviving woman would have over her reproductive life, either actually for a generation of women or hypothetically for a given calendar year, which is the more common usage.

Life expectancy at birth is the average age at death for an actual generation or hypothetically the average age at death implied by the age-specific death rates in a given calendar year, which is the more common usage.

Although pre-transitional fertility was typically high in third-world countries, its levels were far below the hypothetical biological upper limit for a population, which is around 15 to 17 births per woman. The contraceptive effects of prolonged breast-feeding, often combined with taboos on sex while breast-feeding, led to long birth intervals and reduced fertility. Abortion was also important, and sometimes the practice of coitus interruptus had an important effect. In some settings, marriage patterns also limited fertility, although not as strongly as in western Europe. At the aggregate level, population growth throughout the regions of the world was slow over the past millennium, but there was a puzzling similarity in long swings about the growth path, such as stagnation in the fourteenth and seventeenth centuries and more rapid growth in the fifteenth and eighteenth centuries. While exchanges of disease through exploration and trade may have played some role, global climatic change was probably the main driving force.

2.3.1. Fertility Declines and Population Growth

The classic demographic transition starts with mortality decline, followed after a time by reduced fertility, leading to an interval of first increased and then decreased population growth and, finally, population aging.

2.3.2. Mortality Declines

The beginning of the world's demographic transition occurred in northwest Europe, where mortality began a secular decline around 1800. In many low-income countries of the world, the decline in mortality began in the early twentieth century and then accelerated dramatically after World War II. The first stage of mortality decline is due to reductions in contagious and infectious diseases that are spread by air or water. Starting with the development of the smallpox vaccine in the late eighteenth century, preventive medicine played a role in mortality decline in Europe. However, public health measures played an important role from the late nineteenth century, and some quarantine measures may have been effective in earlier centuries. Improved personal hygiene also helped as income rose and as the germ theory of disease became more widely. There are cases in which fertility declined first, notably the United States and France.

Famine mortality was reduced by improvements in storage and transportation that permitted integration of regional and international food markets, smoothing across local variations in agricultural output. Secular increases in incomes led to improved nutrition in childhood and throughout life. Better-nourished populations with stronger organ systems were better able to resist disease. Life expectancy is still positively associated with height in the industrial country populations, plausibly reflecting childhood health conditions.

The high-income countries of the world have largely attained the potential mortality reductions due to reductions in infectious disease and increases in nutrition. In recent decades, the continuing reduction in mortality is due to reductions in chronic and degenerative diseases, notably heart disease and cancer. In the later part of the century, publicly organised and funded biomedical research has played an increasingly important part, and the human genome project and stem cell research promise future gains. Many low-income populations did not begin the mortality transition until some time in the twentieth century. However, they then made gains in life expectancy quite rapidly by historical standards.

2.4. Fertility Transition

Between 1890 and 1920, marital fertility began to decline in most European provinces, with a median decline of about 40 percent from 1870 to 1930. The preceding decline in mortality may have been partly responsible, although it cannot explain the timing.

Most economic theories of fertility start with the idea that couples wish to have a certain number of surviving children, rather than births per se. If this assumption holds, then once potential parents recognise an exogenous increase in child survival, fertility should decline. However, mortality and fertility interact in complicated ways. For example, increased survival raises the return on postbirth investments in children. Some of the improvement in child survival is itself a response to parental decisions to invest more in the health and welfare of a smaller number of children. These issues of parental investment in children suggest that fertility will also be influenced by how economic change influences the costs and benefits of childbearing.

Bearing and rearing children is time intensive. Technological progress and increasing physical and human capital make labour more productive, raising the value of time in all activities, which makes children increasingly costly relative to consumption goods. Since women have had primary responsibility for childbearing and rearing, variations in the productivity of women have been particularly important. For example, physical capital may substitute for human strength, reducing or eliminating the productivity differential between male and female labour, and thus raising the opportunity cost of children. Rising incomes have shifted consumption demand toward non-agricultural goods and services, for which educated labour is a more important input. A rise in the return to education then leads to increased investments in education. Overall, these patterns have several effects: children become more expensive, their economic contributions are diminished by school time and educated parents have higher value of time, which raises the opportunity costs of childrearing. Furthermore, parents with higher incomes choose to devote more resources to each child, and since this raises the cost of each child, it also leads to fewer children. Beyond these tightly modelled theories of fertility, more highly developed markets and governments can replace many of the important economic functions of the traditional family and household, like risk sharing and provision of retirement income, further weakening the value of children.

The importance of contraceptive technology for fertility decline is hotly debated, with many economists viewing it as of relatively little importance. The European fertility transition, for example, was achieved using coitus interruptus. This debate extends from the interpretation of the past to prescriptions for current policy. The Least Developed Countries started from a slightly higher initial level of fertility and started their fertility transition later. Currently, 60 countries with 43 percent of the world's population have fertility at or below the replacement level of 2.1 children per woman. The total fertility rate has fallen well below replacement for almost all the industrialised countries and for many countries of east Asia, including Taiwan, south Korea and China. When fertility declines, it declines most at the youngest and oldest ages and becomes concentrated in the 20s and early 30s. Currently, two-thirds of childbearing occurs between ages 20 and 35 in the Least Developed Countries, whereas 80 percent occurs in this age range in the More Developed Countries. Birth rates above age 35 are only one-seventh as high in the More Developed Countries as in the Least Developed Countries and only one-fifth as high below age 20. Despite this general reduction in fertility at older ages, age at first marriage and first birth are generally moving to older ages throughout the industrial and much of the developing world.

2.4.1. Population Growth Rates

Population growth rates in the More Developed Countries rose about a half percent above those in the Less Developed Countries in the century before 1950. But after World War II, population growth surged in the Less Developed Countries, with the growth rate peaking at 2.5 percent in the mid-1960s, then dropping rapidly. The global population share of the More Developed Countries is projected to drop from its current 20 percent to only 14 percent in 2050. Long-term U.N. projections suggest that global population growth will be close to zero by about 2100. Global population projections are regularly prepared by the United Nations and the U.S. Census Bureau. The method could be described as common sense, informed by careful measurement and inspection of trends and current levels and a distillation of historical patterns of decline for fertility and mortality. The central current projections from the United Nations, which are consistent with some other global projections, anticipate that global population will reach 8.9 billion by 2050 and just below 9.5 billion by 2100-a 50 percent increase from its current size.

2.4.2. Population by Major Development Groups

United Nations' high-low range extends over a very wide interval from 5.2 to 16.2 billion. This great uncertainty must be kept in mind when considering all the projections of fertility, mortality and population size for the twenty-first century. The population projection for the More Developed Countries population is nearly flat, with population decrease in Europe and Japan offset by population increase in the United States and other areas. Most of the projected population increase takes place in the Less Developed Countries, which gain 1.8 billion, or 43 percent. However, the greatest proportional gain comes in the Least Developed Countries with their higher fertility and more rapid growth. These countries gain 1 billion in population, or 151 percent. The relative shares of the three groups will change a good deal over the next 50 years.

2.4.3. Shifts in Age Distribution

The patterns of change in fertility, mortality and growth rates over the demographic transition are widely known and understood. Less well understood are the systematic changes in age distribution that are an integral part of the demographic transition and that continue long after the other rates have stabilised.

In the first phase of the transition, when mortality begins to decline while fertility remains high, mortality declines most at the youngest ages, causing an increase in the proportion of children in the population and raising child dependency ratios, as shown in Panel E. Thus, counter to intuition, mortality decline initially makes populations younger rather than older in a phase that can last many decades and here lasts 70 years. During this phase, families find themselves with increasing numbers of surviving children. Both families and governments may struggle to achieve educational goals for the unexpectedly high number of children.

Next, as fertility declines, child dependency ratios decline and soon fall below their pre-transition levels. The working-age population grows faster than the population as a whole, so the total dependency ratio declines. This second phase may last 40 or 50 years. Some analysts have worried that the rapidly growing labour force in this phase might cause rising unemployment and falling capital labour ratios. Others have stressed the economic advantages of having a relatively large share of the population in its working years, calling these a demographic gift or bonus. In India, the bonus occurs between 1970 and 2015. If income per person of working age is unaffected, the decline in dependents per worker would by itself raise per capita income by 22 percent, adding 0.5 percent per year to per capita income growth over the 45-year span. There is considerable controversy about whether this demographic bonus really affects economic development, continuing debates from the 1980s.

In a third phase, increasing longevity leads to a rapid increase in the elderly population while low fertility slows the growth of the working-age population. The old-age dependency ratio rises rapidly, as does the total dependency ratio. In India, this phase occurs roughly between 2015 and 2060-and it would last longer if mortality decline were not assumed to cease in the simulation. If the elderly are supported by transfers, either from their adult children or from a public sector pension system supported by current tax revenues, then a higher total dependency ratio means a greater burden on the working-age population. To the extent that the 9 In some studies, the boundary for childhood is taken to be 18 or 20, and for working ages it may be taken to be 60. Any boundary is arbitrary, as is the equal weighting of children and elders in forming these ratios.

At the end of the full transitional process for India, the total dependency ratio is back near its level before the transition began, but now child dependency is low and old-age dependency is high. Presumably, mortality will continue to decline in the twenty-first century, so that the process of individual and population aging will continue. No country in the world has yet completed this phase of population aging, since even the industrial countries are projected to age rapidly over the next three or four decades. In this sense, no country has yet completed its demographic transition.

2.4.4. Lower Fertility and Longer Life Expectancy

Both low fertility and longer life contribute to the aging of the population. But the implications of these factors for causes of shifts in the population distribution and for how society might react to the aging of the population are rather different. When population aging is due to declining fertility, it raises the share of the elderly population without altering the remaining life expectancy of older individuals. Such aging reflects a choice made by individuals to raise fewer children. The desire to have fewer children may be related to the rise of public sector pensions, which disconnect old-age support from individual fertility, and may have played some role in causing low fertility in industrial nations.

The Least Developed Countries as a group are in the midst of their fertility decline, which is causing a substantial proportion of their population aging. While lower fertility may go with reduced total parental expenditures on children, it also raises the ratio of elderly to working-age people, other things equal, with no corresponding improvement in health to facilitate a prolongation of working years. For this reason, population aging due to reduced fertility may well impose important resource costs on the population, regardless of institutional arrangements for old-age support. By contrast, population aging due to declining mortality is generally associated with increasing health and improving functional status of the elderly. If low fertility is associated with increased human capital investments per child, then these might lead to longer life for those children eventually.

2.5. Consequences of the Demographic Transition

The three centuries of demographic transition from 1800 to 2100 will reshape the world's population in a number of ways. The obvious changes are the rise in total population from 1 billion in 1800 to perhaps 9.5 billion in 2100-although this long-term estimate is highly uncertain due largely to uncertainty about future fertility. The average length of life increases by a factor of two or three, and the median age of the population doubles from the low 20s to the low 40s. Many More Developed Countries already have negative population growth rates, and the United Nations projects that the population of Europe will decline by 13 percent between now and 2050. But many other changes will also be set in motion in family structure, health, institutions for saving and supporting retirement and even in international flows of people and capital.

At the level of families, the number of children born declines sharply and childbearing becomes concentrated into a few years of a woman's life. When this change is combined with greater longevity, many more adult years become available for other activities. The joint survivorship of couples is greatly increased, and kin networks become more intergenerationally dense, while horizontally more sparse. These changes appear to be quite universal so far. However, whether childbearing is concentrated at younger ages or at older ages and whether age at marriage rises or falls seems to vary from setting to setting, and patterns are still changing even in the populations farthest along in the transition. Parents with fewer children are able to invest more in each child, reflecting the quality-quantity trade-off, which may also be one of the reasons parents reduced their fertility.

The processes that lead to longer life may also alter the health status of the surviving population, but the change could go either way. For example, mortality decline may permit less healthy or more disabled people to live longer, thereby raising age-specific disability rates. Alternatively, the decline in damage from trauma and disease in earlier life may reduce rates of disability and illness as people age. For the United States, it appears that years of life added by declining mortality are mostly healthy years, and that at any given age, the health and functional status of the population are improving. Apparently, years of healthy life are growing roughly as fast as total life expectancy, although this is more clearly true for years free of mild disability than severe. In other industrial populations, the story is more mixed, and no general conclusion is yet possible. Trends in health, vitality and disability are of enormous importance for the economic and social consequences of aging and, indeed, for human welfare more broadly.

The economic pressures caused by the increasing proportion of elderly are exacerbated in the More Developed Countries by dramatic declines in the age at retirement, which for U.S. men fell from 74 years in 1910 to 63 years in 2000. Generous public pension programmes permitting early retirement, combined with heavy implicit taxes on those who continue working, have played an important role in causing earlier retirement in industrial nations since the 1960s. The growing ratio of retirees to workers is bringing various policy responses. So-called "parametric" reforms tinker with pay-as-you-go defined benefit programmes, reducing benefits, raising taxes and eliminating the incentives for early retirement. Sweden, Italy and some other European countries have introduced "notional defined contribution" pension systems, whereby pay-as-you-go systems mimic defined contribution programmes, removing incentives for early retirement and passing on to individual retirees the financial risks of rising longevity. Other countries, particularly in Latin America, are making the painful transition to funded public systems. Often these policy changes encounter fierce opposition from workers, but population aging makes reform inevitable. In some countries, like the United States, population aging will generate more intense financial pressures on publicly funded health care systems than it does on pension systems. Overall, the proportion of U.S. GDP spent on government programmes for the elderly is projected nearly to triple over the next 75 years without reforms, while the public expenditure shares for the children and working age people remain relatively flat.

2.6. Conclusion

Population aging, together with the growth of age-related public transfer systems for pensions, education and health, creates massive positive fiscal externalities to childbearing. In aging high-income nations with generous support for the elderly, the net present value of future taxes minus benefits for an incremental birth may be several hundred thousand dollars, giving governments a powerful incentive to encourage childbearing. In developing countries with younger populations and public programmes focused on children, the fiscal externalities and incentives run in the opposite direction.

At the international level, there are intriguing issues about the extent to which the flow of people and capital across borders may offset these demographic pressures. As population growth has slowed or even turned negative in the More Developed Countries, it is not surprising that international migration from third world countries has accelerated. Net international migration to the More Developed Countries has experienced a roughly linear increase from near-zero in the early 1950s to around 2.3 million per year in the 1990s. Of course, these net numbers for large population aggregates conceal a great deal of offsetting international gross migration flows within and between regions.

Population aging may cause declining aggregate saving rates, but with slowing labour force growth, capital/labour ratios will probably rise nonetheless and profit rates fall, particularly if there is a move toward funded pensions. Capital flows from the More Developed Countries into the Less and Least Developed Countries might help to keep the rate of return earned on pension funds from falling. However, simulations indicate that exporting capital to the younger Less Developed Economies would help the industrial economies only slightly. The much smaller size of third-world economies would limit the gains.

Dramatic population aging is the inevitable final stage of the global demographic transition, part and parcel of low fertility and long life. It will bring serious economic and political challenges. Nonetheless, life in aging, capital-intensive and culturally diverse high-income countries should be pleasant, provided our institutional structures are sufficiently flexible to allow us to adapt our life cycle plans to the changing circumstances and provided we are willing to pay for the health care and the extended retirement that we apparently want.

References

Beaver, S. E., *Demographic Transition Theory Reinterpreted,* Lexington, MA: Lexington Books, 1975.

Chesnais, J. C., *The Demographic Transition: Stages, Patterns and Economic Implications,* trans. E. Kreager and P. Kreager. Oxford, UK: Clarendon Press, 1992.

Livi-Bici, M., *A Concise History of World Population,* trans. C. Ipsen. Malden, MA: Blackwell, 1992.

____________ *The Population of Europe,* trans. C. De Nardi Ispen and C. Ispen. Malden, MA: Blackwell, 1999.

3

Population Growth in India

3.1. Introduction

India is often described as a collection of many countries held together by a common destiny and a successful democracy. Its diverse ethnic, linguistic, geographic, religious, and demographic features reflect its rich history and shape its present and future. No fewer than 16 languages are featured on Indian rupee notes. It is also only the second country to achieve a population of 1 billion. While it is an emerging economic power, life remains largely rooted in its villages. Only a small fraction of Indians are benefiting from the country's expanding industrial and information sectors. India has more people than Europe, more than Africa, more than the entire Western Hemisphere. India's population will exceed that of China before 2030 to become the world's most populous country, a distinction it will almost certainly never lose. Just one group, Indian boys below age 5, numbers 62 million-more than the total population of France. India's annual increase of nearly 19 million contributes far more to annual world population growth than any other country.

Although the region has a rich and ancient history, present-day India is a relatively new nation. India gained independence from British rule in 1947, after decades of struggle against the former colonial power. The country was then partitioned into primarily Hindu India and Muslim Pakistan. The eastern part of Pakistan is today's Bangladesh. In the largest mass migration ever recorded, millions of Hindus left Pakistan to resettle in India, as millions of Muslims moved from India to Pakistan. The upheaval of the partition also unleashed a period of horrific violence between Hindus and Muslims, and sporadic conflicts between

Hindus and Muslims and between India and Pakistan continue to this day.

At independence, India consisted of provinces defined by the British, along with more than 500 princely states whose territory was ultimately taken over by the new Indian government. Boundaries for today's states were largely drawn along language lines after independence. In the 21st century, India is a federal republic comprised of 28 states and seven union territories. States and union territories are split into 593 districts and 5,564 subdistricts. New states are created periodically to ease the burden of governing as their populations grow or to provide separate states for ethnic and tribal groups. Three new states were created in 2000 when Jharkhand was split from Bihar, Chhattisgarh was cut from Madhya Pradesh, and a few mountain districts were carved out of Uttar Pradesh to form the state of Uttaranchal. Part of Kashmir, along the northwestern border with Pakistan, is occupied by Pakistan, although India considers it Indian territory. Disputes over this territory have spawned intense political battles and terrorism.

In the far north, India is dominated by the grand sweep of the Himalayas, Hindu Kush, and Patkai mountain ranges, which soon give way to the vast and fertile Indo-Gangetic plain of the north, fed by such major rivers as the Ganges and Yamuna. Here are located many of India's most populous states such as Haryana, Delhi, Uttaranchal, Uttar Pradesh, Bihar, Jharkhand, and West Bengal. Mughuls invaded from Afghanistan in the 16th century, leaving a mark on the architecture, food, and dress of northern India still discernable today. Hindi, India's official language of government, is spoken in much of the north, and the area from Rajasthan to Bihar is often referred to as the "Hindi Belt." This region, which contains just over 40 percent of the national population, is known for high birth and death rates, low literacy levels, and endemic rural poverty.

Mountain ranges divide north from south, marking the beginning of the Deccan Plateau that makes up much of southern India. The north/south division also marks enormous socioeconomic differences. In contrast to high illiteracy, rapid population growth, and poor health common in the north, the southern states of Kerala, Karnataka, and Tamil Nadu are known for high literacy levels, long life expectancy, and low birth rates. Throughout history, the south had more contact with an outside world attracted by its profitable spice trade. Trade and interaction with foreign people encouraged literacy and introduced a diversity of religions. Although Hinduism predominates throughout the region, Kerala, on the southwestern coast, has one of the highest proportions of both Christians and Muslims in India. That state has also historically been one of India's most advanced in terms of women's rights and education levels. Northeast India, barely connected to the rest of the country by a narrow strip of land known as the Siliguri, or "Chicken's Neck," consists of seven smaller states, some carved out of the state of Assam, which are ethnically closer to Southeast Asia than to the rest of India.

3.2. Population Change

The Indian subcontinent has long been one of the world's most populous regions, but as in many of today's developing countries, population growth took off in the 20th century. India began the century with a population of about 238 million and ended it with 1 billion. India added another 100 million by 2006, when its population reached an estimated 1.1 billion. This phenomenal growth followed a century of relatively stable population size, according to most historical estimates. Scholars differ in the historical estimates of the region's population, but many assume that the population was roughly 200 million in the early 1800s. India's population total remained more or less static during the 19th century, reflecting a slender balance of births over deaths. Growth slowly accelerated in the late 1800s. By 1871, India's population had reached 255 million. The first population census was conducted in 1872, and a census has been taken every decade since.

India's population growth pattern is typical for a high-fertility and high-mortality country in that population grew quite slowly, even declining in the early 20th century. High birth rates were counterbalanced by high death rates, along with periodic famines, outbreaks of lethal diseases such as cholera and smallpox, and endemic parasitic diseases such as malaria. But epidemics and famines receded in the first half of the 20th century. The year 1921 is often referred to as the "Year of the Great Divide," because it marked the shift from a pattern of relatively static population size to one of steady and often rapid increase. As the mid-20th century approached, growth began to accelerate as the more serious threats to public health waned: Death rates fell but birth rates remained high. India's population growth rate peaked between the 1971 and 1981 censuses, but growth in absolute numbers has not yet peaked. The country added 16 million people annually in the 1980s and 18 million annually in the 1990s until the present. India's population growth slowed as the birth rate gradually declined beginning in the late 1960s. Since the early 1970s, the birth rate has fallen from just under 40 births per 1,000 population to 24 per 1,000 in 2004. This decline reflected the concerted effort by the government to slow population growth.

3.2.1. Mortality

India's mortality has declined at a sluggish rate. In the early 1970s, the infant mortality rate (IMR) was about 130 deaths to infants under age 1 per 1,000 live births. By 2004, the IMR declined to about 58. In recent years, the pace of improvement has quickened. Maternal mortality has also declined since the 1970s, although at 540 maternal deaths per 100,000 births in 2000, the rate remains higher than in many other less-developed countries, and nearly 10 times higher than in China. Declining death rates, especially among infants and young children, boosted the average life expectancy for Indians from about 50 years in the early 1970s to 63 years for the 1999-2003 period. The national average is similar to levels in neighbouring Bangladesh, Nepal, and Pakistan. Yet, life expectancies are above 70 years in some Indian states such as Kerala, and other Asian countries, including Sri Lanka and Thailand, and are 80 or above in Singapore and Japan, suggesting there is considerable room for improvement in India. A substantial fall in mortality could boost population growth unless accompanied by further declines in the birth rate. Life expectancy at birth varies by nearly 20 years among Indian states, ranging from 57 years in Madhya Pradesh to 74 in Kerala. These vast differences reflect a large gap among states in education and access to health services.

3.3. Indian Census

Often called the largest administrative exercise in the world, India's census is a truly monumental exercise that involves 2 million enumerators and supervisors. In the year before the census, enumerators canvass the entire country listing every dwelling-whether a house or temporary structure. This list serves as a basis for planning enumerator assignments and other organisational needs. The 2001 Census population questionnaire featured 23 questions for people in households, including a new question on women's work as an economic activity.

In 2001, provisional population totals were released only three weeks after the census date-March 1-an amazing feat considering the size of the country. The Indian censuses have very good coverage by global standards. After the 1991 Census, the Registrar General's office estimated that the census undercount was about 1.8 percent of the population. Detailed data from the census highlight the fact that many Indians do not know their exact birth year and often report an approximate age rounded to a "0" or "5." As shown in the figure, this rounding causes pronounced heaping of census data by age, as seen in the bars jutting out from the population pyramid at ages ending in 0, and to a lesser extent, ages ending in 5.

Census data also reveal that females, particularly in younger ages, are often missing from census figures. In Uttar Pradesh in 2001, the number of females below age 25 is about 6 million fewer than what would be expected in a "normal" age-sex distribution. Some of this female deficit reflects sex-selective abortions by parents who want to avoid having a girl and the omission of female household members from the census count.

3.3.1. Sample Registration System (SRS)

India is one of a few developing countries that publish annual birth and death rates. Since the 1970s, its Sample Registration System (SRS) has collected data on births and deaths from sample villages and from sample census blocks in urban areas. India publishes annual estimates of birth, death, and infant mortality rates; life expectancy; and other key measures for the nation and most states. Less detail is provided for smaller states because of insufficient sample sizes. The quality of SRS estimates has improved over the years, and the SRS provides valuable data for officials and planners who rely on population data. In 2004, the SRS covered 7,597 sample units comprising 1.3 million households and 6.7 million people.

3.3.2. National Family Health Surveys

The National Family Health Surveys (NFHS), a part of the global Demographic and Health Survey (DHS) program, have provided a wealth of information on a wide variety of sociodemographic topics. The NFHS produce measures of fertility, contraceptive use, childbearing desires, the status of women, infant mortality, immunisation coverage, use of iodized salt, reproductive health, knowledge of HIV and AIDS, housing, and other valuable data. The first two surveys were taken in 1992-1993 and 1998-1999. With a sample size of nearly 90,000 women of childbearing age, the NFHS provides detailed analyses down to the state level. A third NFHS being conducted in 2006 has an even larger sample size, will include men, and will test participants for HIV infection.

3.3.3. India's Population by Sex

The history of high birth rates has kept India's population relatively young: In 2005, about 36 percent of the population was below age 15 and just 4 percent was age 65 or older. The broad-based age and sex population "pyramid" taken from United Nations projections shows this youthfulness clearly. More than half the population is below age 25. The young population virtually guarantees further growth, as these young people produce their own families, who will also require additional schools, jobs, and housing.

3.3.3.1. Sex ratio at birth

One of the most striking features of India's population profile is its abnormally high ratio of males to females, particularly at young ages. While about 105 boys are born for every 100 girls in most countries, the ratio is about 113 per 100 in India, and it ranges up to 129 per 100 in some states. This skewed ratio has been increasing. The overriding explanation is the abortion of female fetuses. While abortion has been legal in India since 1972, sex-selective abortion has been illegal since 1994. However, the government has not effectively enforced the ban. The practice has increased, especially in wealthier states, such as Haryana and Punjab, and in urban areas, where couples are more likely to have access to the prenatal tests to determine their fetus' sex. The government has redoubled efforts to enforce the ban in recent years in the face of growing alarm at the frequency of female feticide.

Efforts to stem the practice of sex-selective abortion include a broader campaign to improve the status of women and to encourage parents to value daughters as well as sons. In districts where son preference is especially strong, initiatives involve medical professionals, religious leaders, schools, television shows, and politicians. A "Save a Girl Child" campaign highlights the achievements and value of young girls. This desire to enhance the value of daughters was behind the government's decision to choose a baby girl as India's official "billionth baby," born in Safdarjung Hospital in New Delhi on May 11, 2000.

Delhi is launching a "Girl Child Protection Scheme" campaign under which 5,000 rupees (US$111) will be deposited in the name of every girl born in a government hospital or maternity home. The money and accrued interest will be given to the girl when she reaches 18 and completes a specified level of education. The Punjab government will give a reward of 250,000 rupees (US$5,556) to communities that achieve a target sex ratio among recorded births. Jalahmazra village in Nawashahr, Punjab, received this reward in 2006.

3.4. Geographic Diversity

The Indian population is heavily concentrated in the broad fertile northern plains. Historically higher birth rates in the northern states continue to shift a larger share of India's population growth northward. Four northern states-Bihar, Madhya Pradesh, Rajasthan, and Uttar Pradesh-often referred to as the "BIMARU" states, accounted for 40 percent of India's population, but 47 percent of the country's population growth between 1991 and 2001. Uttar Pradesh, with 166 million people in 2001, is by far India's most populous state and is larger than Pakistan and Bangladesh. Fertility decline has been most dramatic in southern states, and those states contribute less and less to India's annual population growth. Andhra Pradesh, Karnataka, Kerala, and Tamil Nadu accounted for 22 percent of the country's population in 2001, but contributed only 14 percent of its population growth. This disparity is certain to increase.

3.4.1. Lives in Villages

Although many Westerners associate Indian life with teeming megacities, as the country's registrar general said in 2005, "India lives in its villages." A large majority of Indians live in relatively small localities and are engaged in farming or some activity related to farming. In 2001, the average Indian lived in a village of about 4,200 people; 72 percent of India's total population was classified as rural, and 58 percent of workers were engaged in agriculture. Just 11 percent of Indians lived in large cities of 1 million or more residents. Many Indians who live in relatively populated areas are classified as rural because their communities are highly dependent on agriculture and lack the population density required for the official urban designation.

In general, India classifies communities as urban if they have at least 5,000 people; a population density of at least 400 people per square kilometer (1,000 per square mile); and less than 25 percent of the male labour force engaged in agriculture. Accordingly, many of the 16 percent of Indians living in places with 5,000 to 19,999 people are classified as rural. Throughout most of India, rural residents have lower educational levels, higher mortality and fertility, higher poverty, and fewer modern amenities than urban residents. Rural-to-urban migration has been much slower than in Latin America and in other world regions. Most Indians live their entire lives within a relatively limited geographic area.

3.4.2. Urban India

Before 1951, defining an urban area was left entirely to the discretion of local authorities, leading some demographers to joke that "in the pre-independence era, some princely states of India, in order to lay a claim to respectability, were inclined to treat any habitation with a lamppost as an urban centre." The definition of an urban place in India has varied, but now is similar to that used in most other developing countries. In addition to the criteria mentioned above, some places-centers of government, for example-are officially designated as urban regardless of their other characteristics. As in other countries of South Asia, India's urban population has grown relatively slowly for the last century. The percentage of Indians living in urban areas rose from 11 percent in 1901 to 28 percent in 2001.

3.4.3. Indian Megacities

The world has about 20 megacities-urban areas with 10 million or more people. Three are in India: Delhi, Kolkata (Calcutta), and Mumbai. Delhi is one of the world's oldest cities and has been India's capital since 1911. Kolkata, Mumbai, and Chennai (Madras) were established under colonial rule. Kolkata was founded as a port for the British East India Company while Mumbai was founded by Portuguese colonialists. India's fourth-largest city, Chennai, in the southern state of Tamil Nadu, was another British creation, beginning as Ft. George. Delhi is the world's fastest-growing megacity, adding nearly one-half million people per year. Although the city has long since expanded beyond the original inhabited area, it still has room to grow both within its borders and in adjacent suburbs.

Mumbai, located on a long peninsula in Maharashtra state, has had to build up rather than out and available land is now virtually nonexistent. Large cities have sprung up across the bay on the mainland, expanding the greater Mumbai area. With its tall buildings and status as a financial capital, downtown Mumbai gives some visitors the feel of a Manhattan. At partition, Kolkata (the Bengali name for Calcutta) became the capital of the Indian state of West Bengal, while the eastern half of Bengal became East Pakistan and, in 1971, Bangladesh. When Kolkata-the commercial centre of Bengal province-was cut off from the rest of its population, Bangladesh was left largely dependent on subsistence agriculture, and remains one of the world's poorest countries today.

Other major cities include Bangalore, the capital of Karnataka state with its gleaming Indian headquarters of such companies as IBM and Intel; and Hyderabad, capital of Andhra Pradesh state and another important centre of India's growing computer industry.

Slum Populations More than 40 million urban Indians live in areas classified as slums-a number roughly equal to the population of Spain. Slums (jhuggis) are defined as any area designated as such by a state or local government or any "compact area of at least 300 population or about 60 to 70 households of poorly built, congested tenements in [an] unhygienic environment usually with inadequate infrastructure and lacking in proper sanitary and drinking water facilities."

3.4.4. Urban and Rural Population

Most inhabitants of slums came to the city in hopes of earning some income, no matter how meager. Other slum dwellers may, in fact, have paying jobs but live in the slums because of a severe shortage of other housing. Nearly three-fourths of slum residents are literate (73 percent), just below the 81 percent literacy reported among the general population in states reporting slums. Slightly more than one-half of men living in slums were reported as working, about the same as among the general population. Yet women who live in slums are less likely than the average to be working: just 12 percent of women compared with 26 percent among women in the total population of those states in 2001. Slums are by definition illegal, usually rising on a piece of empty government or private land in less desire. The strong preference for sons and low value of women in India have long fostered an unusually high ratio of men to women, but the imbalance has reached alarming levels. The deficit of young girls among children under age 7 increased in all the major states except Kerala between 1991 and 2001, as shown in the figure.

The sharpest increases occurred in an almost contiguous belt extending from northwest India to parts of Rajasthan. In the past, India's high sex ratio has been attributed to better nutrition and health care for males than for females, resulting in higher female death rates from early infancy up to the mid-thirties. Also, women and girls were more likely to be missed in censuses and surveys, so part of the high sex ratio was created by omission rather than an actual imbalance. But record keeping and health care have improved-child mortality has fallen faster for girls than for boys-so these traditional explanations do not account for the recent increase in the sex ratio. Abortion of female fetuses appears to be the primary cause. Some expectant parents rely on sonograms and other medical tests to determine the sex of the fetus, and abort the females.

Declining fertility rates are part of the story-couples are choosing to have fewer children, but they want to ensure that at least one of them is a boy. The ideal family is often described as consisting of two sons and one daughter. Recent studies show that couples are likely to seek sex-selective abortion only after they have produced one or two daughters and no sons. The advent of portable sonogram equipment and access to abortion have made it easy for parents who want to avoid having more daughters.

In 1994, the Prenatal Diagnostics Techniques Act made sex determination and sexselective abortion illegal, but it was rarely enforced and the sex ratio kept rising. Growing public awareness and concern, along with stricter amendments passed in 2002, do not appear to have curtailed the practice. During a routine sonogram, technicians can reveal the fetus' sex to parents through gestures or code words-nothing is written down, so it is hard to prosecute. Women expecting a daughter can then get an abortion for another reason. The practice is difficult to stamp out and couples are still aborting female fetuses in alarming numbers. New methods-possibly even home test kits-to determine a fetus' sex will make it even easier to circumvent the law. And, expectant parents will pay enough to tempt doctors and health workers to ignore the laws. In fact, the sex ratio is more skewed among children in wealthier than in poorer families, suggesting that the ability to pay for sex determination and abortion are important factors. The policies to counteract sex-selective abortion must go beyond cracking down on health workers, because these practices can easily occur outside the law. Policies must attack the cultural bias against women that is the root of the problem.

3.4.4.1. Infrastructure Development in Rural and Urban Areas

Bartering goods and services is common, so much everyday commerce is missed by official statistics. Among those who use cash, rural residents spend more than one-half of their money on food. Although India has participated in the communications revolution, access to telephones and computers within the home has been very limited, especially in rural areas. In 2001, about 11 percent of Indian households had a telephone (including cell phones), but this varied from 23 percent in urban areas to 4 percent in rural areas. Many Indians have access to public telephone services, but the advent of cell phones could bring access to millions more within a relatively short time. Although still concentrated in urban areas, the number of cell phone subscribers (including businesses) has surged in recent years, from 4 million in 2000 to 76 million in 2005. Despite the growing importance of the computer industry to India's economy, few Indians have access to a computer at home. In 2001, less than 3 percent of Indians in urban areas, and less than 1 percent in rural areas, had a computer at home. Even fewer had Internet connections.

Internet access is burgeoning outside the home in urban areas, however, in "cybercafes," schools, and businesses. Some multinational technology companies see India as a potentially lucrative market for personal computers, especially as hardware prices decline and Internet access expands. One consumer item that clearly stands out is television, owned by one in three households. Roughly half of households in both rural and urban areas have some means of private transportation, although bicycles predominate. There has been a surge in the number of privately owned vehicles in recent years, but car ownership is uncommon, especially in rural areas. By 2003, the number of registered cars and vans (including jeeps, used primarily in rural areas) rose to 8.6 million, up from 1.2 million in 1981. The fact that Delhi's 1.1 million cars represent 17 percent of the nation's total while the state has but 1.3 percent of the country's population illustrates the dominance of the major metropolitan areas in car ownership. Ownership of two-wheel vehicles has grown more rapidly than four-wheel vehicles in the past decade.

3.4.5. Household Amenities

3.4.5.1. Increasing Private Motor Vehicles

India's society is deeply rooted in religion, language, and tradition. Religion and conflicts among religious and cultural groups are fundamental forces in Indian life that bear on economic and educational disparities, the division of political power, the traditional role of women, and on the demographic profile of the country. At the 2001 Census, just over 80 percent of Indians practiced Hinduism, one of the world's oldest religions. Muslims are second, with 13 percent. The balance consists of Christians, Sikhs, Buddhists, Jains, and others, such as Parsis. The ongoing conflicts between the Hindu majority and Muslim minority-which occasionally erupt in violence-fuel fears about the long-term effects of demographic changes that could shift the balance of the two groups in some states. Muslims have higher fertility and are growing at a slightly faster rate than Hindus. While a relatively small minority nationally, Muslims make up one-quarter or more of the population in Kerala, West Bengal, Assam, and Jammu and Kashmir, as shown by 2001 Census results. With higher fertility and a more rapid growth rate, the Muslim percentage is slowly increasing nationally. Between 1991 and 2001, the Muslim percentage in India increased from 12 percent to 13 percent. The Muslim percentage increased slightly more in many states, for example, it rose from 23 percent to 25 percent in Kerala, from 28 percent to 31 percent in Assam, and from 18 percent to 19 percent in Uttar Pradesh. Hinduism has been a unifying force throughout India's history. With its many holy days, festivals, and caste system, it defines life for the great majority of Indians. Several other religions, although with much smaller percentages of the population, have also had an important influence in some regions. Sikhs, for example, whose religion branched off from Hinduism, are native to Punjab state. They are generally credited with turning that region's marginal cropland into "India's granary." The importance of Hindu traditions is manifested in India's deeply rooted caste system, which continues to play a key role in the organisation and stratification of Indian society.

The discriminatory aspects of the caste system have been under assault since India's independence in 1947, but the system has been difficult to dislodge, particularly because of its deep roots in ancient texts at the basis of Hinduism, such as the Vedas, and the belief that the creator of the universe, Brahma, also created the four main divisions. Still, the Indian government has attempted to lower caste boundaries and to redress the effects of discrimination against the Dalits. In 1947, well before the landmark civil rights laws in the United States, India established a system whereby a percentage of public-sector jobs and university slots were reserved for certain castes of Dalits. The castes identified were known as Scheduled Castes (SCs) and recognised only among Hindus and Sikhs. The reservation of jobs and university seats was also extended to specific tribal groups (scheduled tribes or STs) that had suffered from discrimination. STs were not necessarily Hindu or associated with a caste, but had a long history of poverty and low educational attainment. In 2006, 15 percent of job vacancies and university seats were reserved for SCs and nearly 8 percent for STs. The reservation policy is not without controversy, in part because of concerns that STs and SCs are not adequately prepared for these positions, and that they prevent more qualified candidates from getting jobs or university seats. Many ST and SC youths grow up in poverty, with limited educational resources, and find it hard to compete with more-educated students in the university setting. A recent Times of India article noted that 2,000 of the 9,000 places reserved for SC/STs in prestigious Delhi.

Literacy and Education Mass education and literacy are a hallmark of modern society. In India, the goal of free and compulsory education through age 14 is provided for under Article 45 of the Constitution. Literacy is defined as the ability to read and write any language, regardless of level of education. In the census, literacy is based on the response of whoever answers the enumerator's questions, nearly always a male household head. Thus, the census figures may overstate the functional literacy levels of the population.

Given the low literacy among Indians at independence, the government has made great progress in educating the population, particularly in the past two decades. The percentage of the population who were literate rose from 16 percent to 65 percent between 1951 and 2001, but this total belies the substantial and persistent gap between men and women. Between 1981 and 1991 the number of illiterate Indians declined, and they were outnumbered by literates for the first time in India's history. Women's Roles and Marriage The gender gap in literacy highlights another important aspect of Indian society and tradition: the generally low status of women. Within a family, girls receive less nutrition and medical care than boys, undermining their health and sometimes leading to premature death. Surveys show that girls are less likely than boys to be immunised against major childhood diseases. And, as literacy figures demonstrate, girls were traditionally less likely to go to school. Marriage is universal in India. Most Indian marriages are arranged by parents, leaving little choice to the couples themselves. Unlike contemporary Western cultures, marriage is seen as more of a family or social duty than a romantic liaison, and the selection of mate and marriage ceremonies are important social and religious events.

The practice of dowry was outlawed in 1961, yet it remains widespread and appears to be gaining importance as a status symbol among wealthier Indians. The amount of the dowry can become a contentious issue for a new bride when her inlaws feel it was insufficient and pressure the bride to secure more from her parents.

The decline in adult mortality can have the opposite effect on fertility rates. With increased longevity for both men and women, fewer women die or are widowed at younger ages, exposing them to the risk of pregnancy for longer periods. The major factor in India's fertility decline in recent decades, however, has been an increase in the use of family planning. Indians have been slow to adopt family planning, and the issue has been fraught with political and social controversy, as explained in the next section. But contraceptive use and family planning are gaining wider acceptance, especially among more-educated women.

3.5. Literacy in India

Population Policies in India justifiably claims to be the first country to adopt an official policy to slow population growth, beginning with the country's first Five Year Plan in 1952. In the 1950s, the country was experiencing accelerated population growth created by declining death rates and high birth rates-a situation shared by many developing countries in that period. Death rates had fallen as these countries gained better public sanitation, widespread immunisation of children, and expanded medical care. But birth rates remained high, pushing population growth to unprecedented heights. Initial efforts to implement a family planning program were rather limited, with a budget of US$1.35 million. The programme began by setting up family planning clinics with the expectation that people would seek out the clinics on their own. But the goal of reducing birth rates through family planning was hampered both by deep-seated traditions that favoured larger families and by the enormous challenge of bringing services to a vast, largely rural population. In the second Five-Year Plan (1956-1961), expenditures for family planning were increased and the idea of incorporating family planning into community-based development programs were introduced. Home visits by family planning workers was expanded in the 1960s to reach even more people. The population program gained status when it was brought under the new Ministry of Health and Family Planning in 1966. The government's concern about the country's population growth was heightened in the 1970s when successive censuses had shown that the rate was rising, despite the policies and investments in family planning. This concern set the stage for the family planning programme's most controversial period. This took place during the National Emergency declared by Prime Minister Indira Gandhi in 1975, partly to thwart her political opposition. With financial support from the central government and the political backing of Mrs. Gandhi's popular son Sanjay, many states adopted coercive measures along with quota systems that resulted in the establishment of the infamous sterilisation camps. In the 1976-1977 programme year, 8.3 million sterilisations, primarily vasectomies, were performed, up from 2.7 million the year before. The abuses and negative publicity generated by the Emergency compromised the reputation of the government family planning programme, and family planning services were suspended. By the 1977-1978 programme year, the number of sterilisations had plummeted to 0.9 million.

The slow decline in India's fertility rate of the previous decade stopped. To distance itself from the negative image of the Emergency, the name of the ministry responsible for family planning was changed to the Ministry of Health and Family Welfare, and remains so to this day. The backlash against the involuntary sterilisations was partly responsible for the defeat of Mrs. Gandhi's party in the next elections. Successive governments-including Mrs. Gandhi herself, who returned to power in 1980 and served until her assassination in 1984-have been careful to emphasise the voluntary nature of the programme.

Following the 1994 International Conference on Population and Development in Cairo, India announced that it was adopting a "target-free" approach in its population policy. This change reflected the spirit of the Cairo conference, which called for greater emphasis on a full program of reproductive health that would be less concerned with specific demographic goals. In reality, this new approach has been applied differently in different areas of the country. In some cases, local clinics found it hard to operate without specific quotas, such as the number of women accepting family planning or for condoms distributed. Some states, such as Andhra Pradesh, continued to offer incentives such as cash, or goods such as transistor radios, for women to agree to sterilisation. In the 1998-1999 period, 67 percent of women ages 25 to 29 in Andhra Pradesh had been sterilised, a remarkably high percentage for women under age 30.

The failure of some states to lower their birth rates also has undermined their political clout in the national legislature. Seats in India's parliament are apportioned among the states according to population size. But giving the rapidly growing northern states more seats was viewed as rewarding them for poor performance in lowering birth rates and contradicting the government's policy to reduce population growth. Accordingly, the Indian Supreme Court has repeatedly frozen the allocation of seats to the population distribution as of 1971. In 2000, the year population reached 1 billion, the government promulgated its first National Population Policy, NPP 2000.27 This policy contained a comprehensive sociodemographic program covering 14 topics such as reducing infant and maternal mortality, promoting later marriage, universal immunisation of children, and preventing the spread of HIV. The policy maintains a commitment to couples' "voluntary and informed choice" of reproductive health services so that replacement level fertility of two children per woman could be achieved by 2010. The need for a separate national population policy had been identified as early as 1983, but was not realised for 17 years. This long delay at least partly reflected fears of a political backlash against family planning, as there had been after the Emergency.

More recently, a debate has been underway regarding elected officials leading by example, willingly or unwillingly, in the practice of family planning. In a number of states, including

Maharashtra, people with more than two children are banned from any elective office from state assemblies to five-member village councils (panchayats). There has been an outcry against this policy as inequitable and too strict, and charges that it will increase, not reduce, female feticide. In the wake of the controversy, Himachal Pradesh state withdrew its two child limit for elected officials in 2005.

3.5.1. Family Planning and Fertility

Despite the obstacles, family planning use did slowly rise in India, from 13 percent of couples in 1970 to 53 percent for the 2002-2004 period. Given the logistical problems of supplying information and services to more than 250 million women of reproductive age, this increase is a remarkable achievement. Women's knowledge of contraception is nearly universal, although knowledge of traditional methods such as rhythm and withdrawal is less common. Most Indian women know about female sterilisation, but other modern methods, such as intrauterine devices (IUDs) or the pill, are much less well known. Female sterilisation remains the most common method of family planning. Female sterilisation rose from 27 percent to 34 percent of contraceptive methods used between NFHS-1 (1992-1993) and the Reproductive and Child Health (RCH) Survey of 2002-2004. Among women familiar with them, "spacing" methods such as the pill and IUD are widely mistrusted for fear of side effects, and female sterilisation is often viewed as the best alternative. Male sterilisation is unpopular; prevalence recorded in the NFHS and other surveys has been declining as older husbands who had been sterilised in the 1970s during the Emergency age out of the sample of women ages 15 to 49.

Contraceptive use is higher in urban than rural areas and increases with a woman's educational attainment. Among religious groups surveyed in NFHS-2, Sikhs and Jains had the highest use, 65 percent, followed by Christians at 52 percent and Hindus at 49 percent. Muslims have the lowest rate of contraceptive use at 37 percent. Contraceptive use was also well below the national average among women from the scheduled tribes (STs) in 1999, but not for women in scheduled castes (SCs).

3.5.2. Fertility Trends

Past trends in birth rates can offer some insight into the future, an important issue given that fertility trends are the primary factor determining India's future population size. As a population transitions from high to low fertility, fertility often declines rapidly to a moderately low rate, then the pace of decline slows as the TFR approaches the replacement level of two children per woman. But the pattern of decline can vary significantly within countries, as illustrated by the trends in the birth rate for two low-fertility states and two high-fertility states between 1971 and 2004. Karnataka and Kerala began at the same level in 1971, when they were already among India's low-fertility states. The rates appeared to plateau during the 1970s-an apparent rejection of family planning after the excesses of the Emergency. But Karnataka's birth rate was stagnant through the 1980s, while Kerala's plummeted. The gap between the two states has narrowed during the early 1990s, but both have plateaued, with no sign that Karnataka's birth rate will fall as low as Kerala's.

3.5.3. HIV and AIDS

India is a low-prevalence HIV/AIDS country, with an estimated 0.9 percent of the adult population ages 15 to 49 infected with HIV. While the rate is relatively low, India has the world's largest number of people of all ages with HIV: 5.7 million in 2005. South Africa is estimated to have a similar, but slightly lower number of HIV-infected people: 5.5 million. South Africa's population is much smaller than India's (47 million compared with 1.1 billion in 2006), but an estimated one-fifth of South African adults are infected with HIV. China, the only country larger than India, has just 0.1 percent of adults infected with HIV, and an estimated 650,000 people of all ages. These estimates, from the Joint United Nations Programme on HIV/AIDS (UNAIDS), have a margin of error because it is impossible to precisely measure the number of HIV-infected people. The estimates of HIV prevalence, and the relative ranking of countries, have always been controversial. India uses a network of "sentinel sites" to evaluate the extent of HIV-infection, a practice followed in most developing countries that lack accurate data on disease.

3.5.3.1. Combating HIV and AIDS

India reacted to the earliest cases of HIV, discovered in 1986 in the port cities of Chennai and Mumbai, by establishing the National AIDS Control Programme. The initial budget was insufficient for the task, and the program did not gain momentum until about 1992. State AIDS Cells set up to manage the programme at the local level proved cumbersome, and the programme languished. But an experimental programme established in 1994-the Tamil Nadu State AIDS Control Society-was so successful that it has become the model for other states. State AIDS Control Societies based on the Tamil Nadu programme-which drew members from all government departments and from non-governmental organisations-have been established in 32 states and union territories.

HIV is spreading largely through sexual activity, although intravenous drug use plays a major role in the two high-prevalence northeastern states of Nagaland and Manipur. Four other states-Andhra Pradesh, Karnataka, Maharashtra, and Tamil Nadu-are considered to be high-prevalence states because the prevalence measured at ANC sites has been 1.0 or above. HIV-prevention campaigns are often aimed at truckers -who spend long periods away from home and on the road. The prevalence is higher along major highways. Commercial sex workers, another high-risk group, are more difficult to locate because so many do not operate from fixed locations.

HIV programmes in India have been expanding geographically, and include more testing and counselling centers, a new anti-retroviral treatment programme, and expanded publicity. TV spots with popular sports figures and actors, as well as newspaper advertisements and billboards, are attempting to spread information about how to avoid HIV infection and to reduce the intense discrimination faced by HIV-positive people in India. The government's campaign, assisted by major support from foreign governments and foundations, has continued to expand, but given the size and diversity of India's population, few countries face a bigger challenge in fighting HIV.

3.6. Future Population

India's future population size will largely depend upon the future course of the birth rate, particularly in the heavily populated north. UN projections offer one view of India's population future. The low variant sees India growing from 1.1 billion in 2006 to

1.3 billion in 2050. This projection, however, makes the unrealistic assumption that the country's total fertility rate will quickly decline from about 3.0 in 2005 to 2.10 in the 2010-2015 period, and then continue downward to 1.35 by 2030-2035. The medium variant assumes that a TFR of 2.1 children would be reached by 2020-2025 and then level off at 1.85 by 2030-2035, resulting in a 2050 population of 1.6 billion. Finally, the high variant assumes that the TFR would fall from 3.0 to 2.35 by 2030-2035, remaining stationary thereafter. The high variant yields a population of 1.9 billion in 2050.

3.7. Conclusion

Few countries are as complex as India. A visitor to Delhi or Bangalore might leave with the impression that India is rapidly becoming a middle-class country with a consumer-oriented lifestyle. But India remains an essentially rural country steeped in centuries-old social and religious traditions. In its modern cities, large proportions of the population live in officially classified slums. Still, progress on many fronts has been remarkable, if uneven, particularly in light of its vast population. Agricultural production quadrupled during a remarkable transformation of its agricultural sector in the 1960s and 1970s (the "Green Revolution"), which, along with expanded transportation and communications networks, have made famines nearly obsolete. Nonetheless, almost 50 percent of Indian children are malnourished. The expansion of the health care system has raised life expectancy at birth to 63 years from less than 40 years in 1950. But less than half of births are attended by skilled health personnel, and maternal mortality is still high.

During the 20th century, India's population growth awoke from the doldrums as real progress was made against disease and hunger. The quarter-billion of 1900 became the 1 billion of 2000. Slowing such unheard-of growth became a national priority from the nation's beginning, and India can count many successes in that effort. But India's wide social diversity has resulted in very different demographic situations-persistently high fertility in the

Hindi Belt compared with below-replacement fertility in Kerala, for example. Success in one area has not been matched by success in others. India's future population size will depend upon what happens in the heavily populated north. In 2000, India's population reached 1 billion. Now the question of 2 billion arises. Will India become the world's first population "double billionaire?" Such a development is well within mathematical possibility. That is one of India's most compelling future issues.

References

Ashford, Lori S., "New Population Policies: Advancing Women's Health and Rights," *Population Bulletin* 56, no. 1, 2001.

Dyson, Tim, Robert Cassen, and Leela Visaria, eds., *Twenty-First Century India: Population, Economy, Human Development, and the Environment,* New York: Oxford University Press, 2004.

_______________, "India's Population: The Past," in *Twenty-First Century India: Population, Economy, Human Development, and the Environment*, ed., Tim Dyson, Robert Cassen, and Leela Visaria, New York: Oxford University Press, 2004.

ESCAP, *Population of India, Country Monograph Series* no. 10, New York: United Nations, 1982.

Kingdon, Greta et al., "Education and Literacy," in *Twenty-First Century India: Population, Economy, Human Development, and the Environment,* ed. Tim Dyson, Robert Cassen, and Leela Visaria, New York: Oxford University Press, 2004.

Visaria, Leela and Pravin Visaria, "India's Population in Transition," *Population Bulletin,* 40, no. 3, 1995.

Visaria and Visaria, "India's Population in Transition"; and International Institute for Population Sciences (IIPS), *Reproductive and Child Health: District Level Household Survey 2002-04,* Mumbai: Government of India, 2006.

4

Population Density

4.1. Introduction

Traditional measures of urbanisation based on administrative and political geographic units are inadequate to address many questions related to population settlement patterns and ecological issues that arise in recent comparative studies. National differences in the definition of urbanisation and the dependence of those definitions on administrative designations of political subunits have always made crossnational comparisons difficult. In studies of the relationship between population and the environment, these differences are heightened by the ecological emphasis on the natural environment. Urbanisation is usually conceptualised as a characteristic of the population or society, but in ecological studies there is equal interest in defining urbanisation in terms of land use and land cover characteristics. While measurement differences are difficult enough to deal with when comparing the percentage of the population that is urbanised, they are much more likely to cause variation in the percentage of the land area in urban designated areas. The choice of geographic unit of analysis and definitional criteria and methodology can result in varying degrees of "overbounding" or "underbounding," sometimes within the same area.

The differences in overbounding and underbounding that are annoyances in the measurement of population size become major problems for measuring the extent of urban land use. Because ecologists often are interested in how landscapes and the environment have changed over time, changing definitions of urbanisation within a given nation also pose difficulties for analysis. In the U.S., demographic data from past censuses are presented only for administrative and political geographic units.

Identifying degrees of urbanisation in the past is made more difficult by the paucity of population and land use data for small geographic areas comparable to the "patches," or small study areas, that feature in ecological research. The lack of detailed population and spatial information often requires use of cartographic methods for defining urbanisation; that is, reliance on mapped portrayals of urban extent. Lack of census geographic area boundary information also poses problems when linking historical demographic data for urban populations with information relating to environmental processes. Portrayal of populations using point data and depicting urban growth and extent through various modeling procedures can overcome problems relating to lack of boundary information.

Defining levels of urbanisation is made more difficult by the fact that it is both a discrete phenomenon that can be observed and measured in place at a specific time, and a process that occurs across space and time. The difference between urbanisation as a phenomenon and urbanisation as a process creates challenges for researchers and policy makers who base conclusions and decisions on observation and measurement of something that has happened in order to affect changes and develop policies in advance of something that will happen. There is no easy solution to the tension created by this dichotomy. It proposes a population density measure of urbanisation that takes advantage of the detailed data on small area populations and land area available in modern censuses and the increasing availability of statistical manipulations in geographic information systems (GIS). The resulting density distributions offer greater potential for understanding and portraying the ecological effects of urbanisation than do traditional urbanisation measures with the additional advantage of comparative measures that minimise the effects of national differences in urban definitions.

4.2. Population and Land Area

The countries in this study, China, India, and the United States of America, are the world's three most populous countries. In the year 2000, China had an estimated population of 1.261 billion; India had 1.014 billion people; and as of April 1 the population of the United States had reached 281,421,906. While the combined population of these three countries accounts for approximately 42 percent of the world's population, the countries occupy only 15 percent of the world's land area. How these countries handle their land and population relationships will have a major impact on how all nations cope with population pressures on environmental resources. The crudest measure of that relationship is a simple population density measure, that is total land area divided by total population. The three countries differ substantially on their level of population density. In 1998, the world's population density was almost 40 persons per sq. km. The U. S. population density was only 28 persons per sq. km., a level substantially below the world average. The population density in China at 130 people per sq. km. is more than three times the world average, even though vast arid areas in the western part of China are sparsely populated. India is one of the more densely populated countries of the world. Its density of 307 people per square km. puts it at almost eight times the average world population density.

Simple population density can be modified by accounting for low density land set aside for non-residential urban uses, such as industrial, commercial, and retail uses as well as parklands. Calculation of net residential densities yields a more accurate depiction of population densities, but does not present an overall depiction of the extent of urbanisation. In addition to accounting for different kinds of land uses and land covers in the definition of urbanisation and calculation of population densities, we should also consider that patterns of urbanisation differ from one location to another depending on local topography, land use regulations, cultural preferences, and so forth. To be truly useful for ecological researchers, definitions and measurements of urbanisation should be multi-dimensional, taking into account patterns of urban development from one place to another resulting in differences in levels of population density, concentration of residential or commercial uses within specific areas, mixing of residential and commercial land uses, amount of intervening land devoted to non-urban uses, and so forth.

More important than the density of each country as a whole is the spatial variation within the country. To illustrate differences between population density calculated for administrative units and small statistical geographic areas, we have chosen one site in each country that is at or above the average population density of the nation in which it is located. The Pearl River Delta area including the major districts of Guangdong province surrounding Hong Kong, Macau, and the Pearl River has a density of 893 persons per square kilometer and an official urban population of 70 percent. South Florida is 96 percent urban but much of the population is clustered along the coast while much of the inland area reserved for national parks and conservation areas. As a result, the average density is only 172 persons per sq. kilometer. At the other extreme, Kerala with an urban percentage of only 26 percent has a dense system of village settlement that leads to a high average population density of 749 persons per sq. kilometer.

4.2.1. Administratively-based Measures of Urbanisation

Most urban definitions take as a starting point the population living in "urban places." These urban places are primarily administratively defined areas generally with recognised municipal governments. These municipal entities can vary markedly in character as well as in size between nations, within nations, and over time. For example, in the United States, laws pertaining to incorporation and annexation vary from statetostate. In states with relatively liberal annexation laws, municipalities can annex lands with relatively low population densities, lands that otherwise would be considered rural. Such situations tend to result in overbounding of urban population and land area. On the other hand, in states with restrictive annexation policies, state laws make it difficult for municipalities to annex adjacent densely populated territory. As a result, when this occurs outside of Census Bureau-defined urbanised areas, the extent of urbanisation often is under bounded in census publications.

The dependence on administratively defined geography to define urban populations makes comparisons of levels of urbanisation difficult across the three sites. Additional problems are posed by changing definitions over time. In China the municipal definition has been changed repeatedly-the most recent change resulting in the inclusion of a large number of municipal districts with boundaries that extend well into the countryside. In India, urban population includes the population of all "towns" defined as places with a municipal corporation, municipal area committee, town committee, notified area committee, or cantonment board. In the U.S., the Census Bureau's definition of urban areas includes "incorporated places" with populations of 2,500 or more.

4.2.2. Statistically-based Measures of Urbanisation

Statistical agencies have dealt with the limitations imposed by administrative units by modifying urban definitions in various ways. In India, there has been a definitional attempt to include other areas outside of "towns" that met the following qualifications: places having 5,000 or more inhabitants, a density of not less than 1,000 persons per square mile (390 per square kilometer), pronounced urban characteristics, and at least three fourths of the adult male population employed in pursuits other than agriculture. In the United States, the Census Bureau expanded its urban definition in 1950 to include the population in unincorporated places of 2,500 or more and in "urbanised areas" consisting of a central place and the adjacent continuously built-up area (containing a population density greater than 1000 persons per square mile and having a total population of 50,000 or more).

In the United States and other countries there have been attempts to account for decentralisation of settlement and economic activity by defining "metropolitan areas" that include not only urbanised areas and outlying urban places but also surrounding counties that are integrated with these urban centers as measured by substantial amounts of daily commuting, even if many of these areas have densities far too low to be classified as urban. In the U.S., the metropolitan area concept does not represent an alternative urban area definition, but rather identifies a functional area influenced by an urban center of significant population size.

These different administrative and statistical definitions make international and temporal comparisons of urban populations difficult. The measures of urbanisation, average density, and land use give very different pictures of the three case study areas. In fact, given our interest in the relationship between land and population, the traditional measures of urbanisation are not sufficient to represent the spatial distribution issues. The concepts of urbanisation differ between the countries, over time within each country, and between researchers.

Urbanisation can be viewed as a characteristic of the population, as a characteristic of particular kinds of land uses and land covers, as well as a characteristic of social and economic processes and interactions affecting both population and land. Social scientists-demographers generally, but also urban policy analysts, geographers, and others-generally define levels of urbanisation in terms of population densities. Physical scientists-ecologists especially-generally approach definitions of urbanisation from the standpoint of the built environment. To these researchers, density of buildings and impervious surfaces is just as important, if not more important, as population-indeed, urban ecologists often are concerned with changes to the environment as a result of human alteration of the landscape. McIntyre et al. note that among ecologists a wide variety of urban definitions have been used in research, ranging from any human alteration of the landscape to more precise definitions based on density and specified land use characteristics. Alternatively, regional economists, labor analysts, and related researchers might define urban in terms of the functional area integrated with an urban center. For these researchers, urban becomes more of a sociological and functional definition than a structural (density-based) phenomenon. Reconciling these different perceptions of what constitutes urbanisation within a single definition poses challenges for any researcher or statistical agency.

Although the authors do not have the access to the detailed level of census tabulations necessary to refine this method for all sites, an example using South Florida can serve as an exposition of how the method might function. In the U. S. decennial censuses, populations are tabulated by small-area geographical units known as census tracts as well as by administrative boundaries such as counties and towns. Census tracts are drawn so as to include approximately 4000 inhabitants and are thus smaller in densely settled areas than in less densely populated areas. The census results by tract include information on both the population and the land area of each tract. Consequently, it is possible to tabulate density distributions of both the population and the land area. Unfortunately, data with which to assess settlement patterns at similar levels of geographic detail in India and China are limited. However, a very crude idea of how this method might work is across countries can be obtained by using the method for the larger levels of geography (districts) that are published for all three countries.

4.3. Conclusion

Given the availability of data for smaller levels of geography for the India and China sites, this measure of high density areas could be useful in making comparative studies that are less influenced by administrative and statistical differences between the countries located in high density areas that are usually thought of as "urban"-and could provide useful information on the percentage of the land area as well as the percentage of the population. This greater detail on the spatial complexity of each area measured at similar levels of spatial disaggregation could begin to supply the comparative data needed for ecological and other studiés across many different societies and landscapes.

References

Buckwalter, Donald W. and Dean S. Rugg, "Delimiting the Physical City: Disparities Between Various Methods of Calculating Population Density," *Professional Geographer*, 1986,

Crawford, J., W. Acevedo, T. Foresman, J. Buchanan, and W. Prince, "Developing a Temporal Database of Urban Development for the Baltimore/Washington Region," *paper presented at the American Society for Photogrammetry and Remote Sensing annual conference*, Baltimore, MD, 1996.

Foresman, TimothyW., Steward T.A. Pickett, and Wayne C. Zipperer, "Methods for Spatial and Temporal Land Use and Land Cover Assessment for Urban Ecosystems and Application in the Greater Baltimore-Chesapeake Region," *Urban Ecosystems*, 1997.

Goldstein, Sidney, "Urbanization in China, 1982-87: Effects of Migration and Reclassification," *Population and Development Review*, 1990.

Ma, Lawrence J. C. And Chusheng Li, "Development of Towns in China: A Case Study of Guangdong Province," Population and Development Review, 1993.

McIntyre, N.E., K. Knowles-Yanez, and D. Hope, "Urban Ecology as an Interdisciplinary Field: Differences in the Use of 'Urban' Between the, Social and Natural Sciences," *Urban Ecosystems*, 2000.

Mohan, Rakesh, "Urbanization in India's Future," *Population and Development Review*, 1985.

Ratcliffe, Michael R. and Timothy W. Foresman, "Historical Geography, Deep Ecology, and GIS: The View From Baltimore," *paper presented at the Association of American Geographers annual meeting*, Honolulu, HI, 1999.

U. S. Census Bureau, "1990 Census of Population and Housing", *Special Tabulations of Census Tracts*, 1993.

United Nations, *Patterns of Urban and Rural Population Growth*, NewYork, 1980.

Zeng Yi and James Vaupel, "The Impact of Urbanization and Delayed Childbearing on Population Growth and Aging in China," *Population and Development Review*, 1989.

5

Sex Composition of the Population

Sex composition of the human population is one of the basic demographic characteristics, which is extremely vital for any meaningful demographic analysis. Indian Census has the tradition of bringing out disaggregated information by sex on various aspects of population. The first and foremost is the simple count of males and females. Changes in sex composition largely reflect the underlying socio-economic and cultural patterns of a society in different ways. Sex ratio defined here as the number of females per 1000 males in the population, is an important social indicator to measure the extent of prevailing equity between males and females in a society at a given point of time. It is mainly the outcome of the interplay of sex differentials in mortality, sex selective migration, sex ratio at birth and at times the sex differential in population enumeration.

It is natural for an ordinary person to believe that males and females in the population exactly balance each other. Little do they know, how imbalanced the sexes are in different populations across the world. It has been estimated that around the year 2000, the world had 986 females against 1000 males. The sheer weight of the population of Indonesia and Japan, the other Asian countries with low sex ratio appears to be largely responsible for the overall preponderance of males over females in the world.

It is interesting to note that the sex ratio in U.S.A., Indonesia, Russian Federation and Japan has always remained above unity for the last half a century. The most dramatic decline of about 200 points in the sex ratio is seen in the Russian Federation. In U.S.A., it has shown as improvement from 1002 to 1029 in the last fifty years. Bangladesh has shown a continuous improvement in its sex ratio to reach from 880 in 1950 to 953 in 2000. Pakistan and China have also shown an improvement. Thus among the major nations of the world, India is the only exception.

According to the Census of India, 2001, the sex ratio stands at 933 for the country as a whole. This is a welcome improvement from the 1991 Census, which had recorded 927 females for every 1000 males. The sex ratio in the country had always remained unfavourable to females. Moreover, barring some hiccups, it has shown a long term declining trend. The sex ratio at the beginning of the twentieth century was 972 and thereafter showed continuous decline until 1941. In 1951 there was a marginal increase of one point, but thereafter it again dropped for two consecutive decades to reach 930 in 1971. In fact, between 1961-71, the country saw the sharpest decline of 11 points in the sex ratio. Thereafter, it has fluctuated marginally around 930 in successive censuses.

5.1. Sex Ratio in India

While working out the sex ratio for India for the year 2001, the estimated population of entire Kachchh district, Morvi, Maliya-Miyana and Wankaner talukas of Rajkot district, Jodiya taluka of Jamnagar district of Gujarat State and entire Kinnaur district of Himachal Pradesh have been used as the population enumeration of Census of India, 2001 could not be conducted in these areas territories, except Arunachal Pradesh, for which data is not available from 1901 to 1951. In 1901, there were as many as eleven States and Union territories that had sex ratio of more than unity. Among these, except Kerala all other States and Union territories have shown a downward slide. The major States those are largely responsible for the decline in the overall sex ratio in India are Uttar Pradesh, Bihar, Jharkhand, Orissa, Chhatisgarh, Madhya Pradesh, Gujarat, Maharashtra and Tamil Nadu. Although the sex ratio in Punjab has been consistently low, it has shown a longterm upward trend and has not contributed to the overall deterioration in sex ratio of the country.

In Rajasthan, the sex ratio kept fluctuating in a narrow band and always remained at a low level. Haryana, Andhra Pradesh and Karnataka are the States where the sex ratio has remained more or less stagnant. In West Bengal the sex ratio declined sharply from 1901 to 1941 and then made a gradual turnaround on an upward path to reach 934 in 2001. The sex ratio of Indian population has always been of topical interest for the demographers, social scientists, women's groups, research scholars and various planners and policy makers. Several reasons are adduced to explain the consistently low levels of sex ratio and their further decline in the country.

The imbalance in the number of males and females begins in the beginning. It is now a well established law of nature that the males exceed females at the time of birth. It is believed that generally 943-952 female births take place for every 1000 male births, which in effect would mean that there is a deficiency of about 50 females per 1000 males in every birth cohort. Many demographers believe that left on its own, this is an unalterable constant. Some likelihood of differential under registration of female births over time notwithstanding, the data on sex ratio at birth for the past many years as obtained from the SRS is indicative of a larger than usual shortfall in female births as compared to male births. The three years moving average sex ratio at birth worked out for India as a whole for the period 1982-98 leaves around 900. During the decade 1981-90 the SRS sex ratio at birth were above 900 whereas in the succeeding decade it has shown definite sign of a decline below 900. Thus for recent period there is some primary evidence that sex ratio at birth in the country as a whole is possibly lower than the generally accepted range of 943-952 but it needs to be corroborated by some more data.

The overall sex ratio of India is dependent on the sex ratios obtained in different States and Union territories and their relative weights in terms of size of population. The diversity in sex ratio among the States and Union territories is phenomenal. At the Census of India, 2001, the sex ratio among the major States ranged from 861 in Haryana to 1058 in Kerala. In 1991 also, Haryana with a sex ratio of 865 was at the bottom with Kerala (1036) at the top. The changes in sex ratio over time, therefore, are dependent on the changes in the ratios of the individual States and Union territories and their relative share in population.

5.1.1. Sex Ratio of Total Population

While working out sex ratio of child population for 1991 Census in the age group 0-6 and population aged 7 and above for India, the population in the age group 0-6 and population aged 7 and above of areas of Gujarat and Himachal Pradesh affected by natural calamities have been excluded. To make the data comparable with Census of India, 2001, the proportion of child population for 1991 Census in the age group 0-6 and population aged 7 and above shown against Himachal Pradesh for 1991 excludes population in the age group 0-6 and population aged 7 and above of Kinnaur district where population enumeration of Census of India, 2001, could not be conducted due to natural calamity.

5.1.2. Distribution of States

It would be interesting to note that although the number of States and Union territories with the sex ratio less than 916 remains almost the same, the percentage share of this population has declined form about forty one percent to about twenty three percent. Similarly the number of States and Union territories falling within the range of 916-950 marginally alters but the share of this population increased from around twenty nine percent to forty seven percent. The contribution of these two groups of States/Union territories appears to be the plausible reason for the increase in overall sex ratio of India.

It may be noted that the number of States and Union territories with sex ratio of below national average has increased from seventeen in 1991 to eighteen in 2001. In fact the proportion of population in the first category has increased from fifty four percent to about sixty percent. In spite of the increase in the number and relative weight in the first category, the overall sex ratio of the country has improved. It can be observed that the highly populated States like Uttar Pradesh, Bihar, Rajasthan and Madhya Pradesh which together constituted about 34 percent of India's population in 1991 and increased to 36 percent in 2001, lie in the category of below national average. Therefore, the increase in the overall sex ratio is possibly due to the relative larger increase in the sex ratio of these four populous States.

5.2. Conclusion

Although the number of States and Union territories having sex ratio of seven plus population and their share of population have remained more or less same in 1991 and 2001, the number as well as share of the State and Union territories in the range 916 -950 has increased substantially. The number and share of States and Union territories having sex ratio 915 and below has shown a significant decline. Among the possible reasons for increase in sex ratio for the population in the age group seven plus, some contribution due to the increase in the life expectancy of females at a faster pace than males as evidenced from the SRS data cannot be ruled out.

References

Bose, A, "Fighting Female Foeticide - Growing Greed and Shrinking Child Sex Ratio", *Economic and Political Weekly*, 8 Sep., 2001.

Chowdhry, P., "Crisis of Masculinity in Haryana The Unmarried, the Unemployed and the Aged", *Economic and Political Weekly*, 2005.

Dasgupta, J., "National Population Policy 2000: A Critique", *Seminar on the New Paradigm of Development and Sex Selection*, New Delhi, India, 2004.

George, S. M., "Sex selection/determination in India : contemporary developments", *Reproductive Health Matters*, Vol. 10, 2002.

Jha, P., Kumar,R., Vasa P., et al, "Low male-to-female sex ratio of children born in India: national survey of 1.1 million households", The Lancet (online) available at www.thelancet.com, 2006.

Larsen, M and Hatti, N., "Family Structures and Declining Child Sex Ratios in India", *Part of a series within ongoing project Lives at Risk: Discrimination of Female Children in modern India*, Swedish Research Council, Preliminary paper, 2004.

Patel, V., "Adverse Juvenile sex ratio in Kerala", *Economic and Political Weekly*, June, 2002.

Shreeniwas, Sudha, "Family Size, Sex Composition and Children's Education: Ethnic Differentials over Development in Peninsular Malaysia," *Population Studies*, Vol. 51, No. 2, July 1997.

South, S. J., Trent, K., "Sex Ratios and Women's Roles: A Cross-National Analysis", *American Journal of Sociology*, Vol. 93, Issue 5, March 1988.

UNFPA, "Sex Selective Abortions and Fertility Decline: The Case of Haryana and Punjab", New Delhi, India, 2001.

UNICEF Media Centre, "UNICEF endorses multi-faith campaign against female foeticide", Available at: http://www.unicef.org/india/media_1030.html, 2005.

Unisa, S., Prakasam, C.P., Sinha,R.K Bhagat, R.B., "Evidence of Sex Selective Abortion from Two Cultural Settings of India: A Study of Haryana and Tamil Nadu" International Institute for Population Sciences, Mumbai, India, 2003.

Varghese, J. Aruldas, V., & Jeemon P., "Analysis of Trends in Sex Ratio at Birth of Hospitalized Deliveries in the State of Delhi", Christian Medical Association of India, July, New Delhi, India, 2005.

6

Fertility and Mortality

6.1. Introduction

Improvement in the standard of living and health status of the population has remained one of the important objectives in Indian planning. All five-year plans had reflected long term vision consistent with the international aspirations of which India has also been a signatory. These long-term goals have been stressed in National Population Policy, National Health Policy, National Nutrition Policy etc. These goals have to be achieved through improving he access to and utilisation of Health, Family Welfare and Nutrition Services with special focus on under served and under privileged segments of population.

6.2. Fertility Trend

National Family Health surveys provide very useful information on trends in fertility. The median age for female sterilisation has been declining in recent years and is now 26 years, one year earlier than in early 1990's. Even for women below 25 years of age, the proportion getting sterilised has increased to 40% in 1998-99 as against 30% in 1992-93. NFHS has shown that groups within the population that have relatively higher fertility are women from rural, scheduled tribes and scheduled castes and illiterate and Muslim which are required to be targeted taking into account cultural, social, economic and behavioural aspects.

6.2.1. Reproductive Health

Maternal mortality: The maternal mortality rate (MMR) in India remains very high at over 500 per thousand live births. Further there appears to be no sign of decline in MMR with time.

Antenatal care: Use of recommended antenatal care is low, but progress has been made. Coverage for different antenatal services has increased, including tetanus toxoid injections and iron/folic acid supplementation. According to NFHS, Mothers of about two third of the children received at least one antenatal check-up and 44 per cent received full antenatal check-ups as against 62% in 1992-93. For two thirds of these births, mothers received the recommended number of tetanus toxoid vaccinations as against 54% in 1992-93. Mothers receiving iron and folic acid supplementation during pregnancy were about 60% as against above 50% in 1992-93. One-third of births in India took place in a medical facility in 1998-99 as compared to one-fourth in 1992-93. States that performed much below the national average with regard to the provision of recommended components of antenatal care are Bihar, Uttar Pradesh, Madhya Pradesh, Rajasthan and several of the northeastern states.

Breast feeding: According to NFHS, Fifty-five per cent of children under four months of age are exclusively breastfed. The median duration of breast-feeding is slightly over two years, and the median duration of exclusive breast feeding is two months. There has been no increase in median duration of breast feeding but the median duration of exclusive breast feeding showed increase.

Reproductive health problem: According to NFHS, nearly 4 out of 10 currently married women report at least one reproductive health problem viz. abnormal vaginal discharge, symptoms of a urinary tract infection, and pain or bleeding associated with intercourse that could be symptomatic of a more serious reproductive tract infection.

Among these women reporting any reproductive health problem, two-thirds have not seen anyone for advice or treatment. Further, women who seek advice or treatment for reproductive health problems do not usually go to government health professionals. These results suggest a need to expand reproductive-health services and IEC programmes that encourage women to discuss their problems with a health-care provider.

Chronic energy deficiency: Based on NFHS data using weight-for-height index (the body mass index), more than one-third (36 per cent) of women in India are undernourished. Nutritional deficiency is particularly acute for women in rural areas, younger women and women in disadvantaged socioeconomic groups. Women who are undernourished are more likely to have children who are undernourished. The proportion of women undernourished is highest in Orissa (48 per cent) and West Bengal (44 per cent). Obesity is a problem among urban women from households with a high standard of living.

Anemia: Anemia is widespread among women. Overall, 52 per cent of women in India have some degree of anemia and 40 per cent or more of women in every population subgroup are anemic. Anemia is a serious concern for women because it can be an underlying cause of maternal and infant death. It can also increase the risk of premature delivery and low birth weight. The prevalence of anemia is particularly high for scheduled tribe women and poor women. Pregnant women are much more likely than non-pregnant women to be moderately to severely anemic. The anemia levels were much higher by ICMR studies.

Adolescent nutrition: Adolescents who are undergoing rapid growth and development are one of the nutritionally, vulnerable groups who have not received the attention they deserve. Where as under nutrition continues to be a major problem in adolescents, over years there has been some increase in obesity.

6.3. Child Health

Infant and child mortality rate: Where as SRS data show stagnency in IMR levels, as per NFHS the infant mortality rate has shown a decline of over 10 points from the level 78.5 per 1000 live births in 1992-93 to 66.6 in 1998-99. The decline in both neonatal and post neonatal mortality is about the same percentage points and almost of similar magnitude in rural and urban areas. IMR greatly varies with age of mother, spacing with last birth and Antinatal care received. Infant mortality rate are more than two and one-half times as high for women who did not receive any of the recommended types of maternity related medical care than for mothers who did receive all recommended types of care. Infant mortality is almost 50 per cent higher among children born to mothers under age 20 than among children born to mothers age 20-29. Infant mortality is nearly three times as high among children born less than 24 months after a previous birth as among children born after a gap of 48 months or more. The IEC should incorporate appropriate messages based on these.

Immunisation: Immunisation coverage, although far from complete, has improved substantially. According to NFHS-2, 72 per cent of children age 12-23 months have been vaccinated against tuberculosis, 63 per cent have received three doses of the polio vaccine and 51 per cent have been vaccinated against measles. Dropout rates for the series of DPT and polio vaccinations continue to be a problem. Coverage has improved for all major vaccines, but dropouts and measles are still a problem. Among major states, Bihar, Assam, Rajasthan, Uttar Pradesh, and Madhya Pradesh stand out as having lower vaccination coverage levels.

Illness: Illness is common among children in India. As per NFHS-2, thirty per cent of children under age three had fever during the two weeks preceding the survey, per cent had symptoms of ARI, and 19 per cent had diarrhea. The levels are higher as compared to NFHS-1. About two-thirds of the children who had symptoms of ARI or diarrohea were taken to a health facility or health-care provider same as that in NFHS-1. Among children sick with diarrhoea in the two weeks prior to the survey, the proportion who were given some form of ORT varies from 90 per cent in Kerala, 76 per cent in Goa, and 73 per cent in West Bengal to 34 per cent in Rajasthan and 36 per cent in Uttar Pradesh. The proportion given ORS varies from 56 per cent in Goa and 51 per cent in Manipur to only 15-16 per cent in Bihar and Uttar Pradesh.

Anemia among Children: The highest anemia levels among children are in Haryana, Rajasthan, Bihar and Punjab. Nearly three-quarters (74 per cent) of children age 6-35 months are anemic, with very little variation in anemia rates for children in most of the population. In young children, anemia can impair cognitive performance, behavioural and motor development, scholastic achievement, as well as increase susceptibility to infectious diseases.

Undernutrition among children: Little less then half of children under age three years in India are underweight slightly less than that in 1992-93 (53%). Forty-six per cent of children are stunted and 16 per cent are wasted. Undernutrition is much higher in rural areas than in urban areas, and is particularly high among children from disadvantaged socio-economic groups. Undernutrition is most serious among children ages 12 to 35 months. However, there is some improvement vis-a-vis the situation in 1992-93.

6.3.1. Anemia among Children

The highest anemia levels among children are in Haryana, Rajasthan, Bihar and Punjab. In young children, anemia can impair cognitive performance, behavioural and motor development, scholastic achievement, as well as increase susceptibility to infectious diseases. However, there is some improvement vis-a-vis the situation in 1992-93. Nearly three-quarters (74 per cent) of children age 6-35 months are anemic, with very little variation in anemia rates for children in most subgroups of the population.

6.3.2. Under Nutrition among Children

Little less then half of children under age three years in India are underweight slightly less than that in 1992-93 (53%). Forty-six per cent of children are stunted and 16 per cent are wasted. Under nutrition is much higher in rural areas than in urban areas, and is particularly high among children from disadvantaged socio-economic groups. Almost half of children under three years of age are underweight, a measure of short -and long-term undernutrition. A similar percentage are undernourished to the extent that their growth has been stunted (46 per cent). Undernutrition is most serious among children ages 12 to 35 months.

6.3.3. Preference for Sons

Son preference is very strong in states like Uttar Pradesh, Bihar and Rajasthan, which leads to larger families as couples continue to have children until they reach their desired number of sons.

6.3.4. Literacy Levels are Rising

Literacy levels among both women and men have improved. Three out of four men are literate and half of women are literate. Those with literacy skills are better able to access information. Higher female literacy is also associated with lower fertility levels.

6.4. Future of Human Fertility in India

Many factors - social, cultural, economic - influence the timing and speed of the fertility decline response in particular populations. But the remote causal force behind all fertility transitions is mortality decline. This is just as true for the developing world today as it was for historical Europe. But because they have benefited from what is sometimes termed a 'late development effect' changes in contemporary developing countries tend to be faster than was the case in Europe. In all societies women not only give birth to the children, but they also do most of the childcare. Therefore circumstances of high fertility tend to lock them up within the domestic domain. In high fertility societies women's relatively short lives were - and in some places still are - dominated by the responsibilities of childbirth and childcare. But this is not true of places where fertility is low and life expectation at birth (LEB) is high.

A major social-structural adaptation to conditions of persistent low fertility is a weakening of the institution of marriage. For women especially, but also for men, marriage in the sense of a formal lifetime commitment for the having and rearing of children becomes much less important than it used to be. Given such conditions women have more time - and partly because they live longer, more reason - to pursue their lives away from the domestic domain. Consequently, especially in the most developed countries (e.g. of Europe, North America, Japan) levels of gender differentiation have tended to fall. And measures of gender equality tend to be greatest in societies with low fertility.

Fertility decline has been occurring for several decades now. And it is this phenomenon, above all, which is opening up completely new employment and educational prospects for young women. Among the general population there has been a rise in women's share of agricultural employment, and an increase in the average wages they earn. There has also been a fall in male -female wage differentials. The truth is that in rural areas many young men simply do not want to work in agriculture. In contrast, however, young women are often more motivated. These processes are contributing to a reduction in the traditional preference for sons. Consequently Bhanwar Rishyasringa has rightly stated that economic changes are occurring in the country in the direction of empowering women relative to men.

In addition education, plus the mass media, are raising women's aspirations. It is increasingly apparent that young women can lead lives largely independent of men. Of course, these developments are most apparent among the better-off sections of urban Indian society - where many well educated young women see no particular reason to get married and where, with increasing individualism, the incidence of divorce is almost certainly on the rise. Among the growing urban elite many couples are content to have just one child - even if it is a daughter. Women become more like men. Marriage and childbearing become less important. In the long run the only thing that is likely to reverse these trends in the world is some kind of fundamental renegotiation of gender roles - a renegotiation in which (to simplify) men may be required to become more like women.

Several additional points of substantiation and qualification must be made apropos the preceding discussion. It is worth emphasising, for example, that fertility is falling in virtually all of India's states, including the core northern ones. The fertility is falling everywhere is established by both the SRS and analysis of own-child data from the two rounds of the National Family Health Survey (NFHS) which were conducted during 1992-93 and 1998-99. The SRS suggests that total fertility has been falling in most states since the 1970s - in some cases the early 1970s, or perhaps even earlier.

Most forward looking analysts concur that in the next few decades average levels of per capita income and urbanisation will continue to rise in most states (albeit at different rates, expected progress generally being faster in India's south). There may be more deep-seated regional dimensions of South Asian society, which have helped to determine the timing and extent of both socio-economic and demographic progress. Accordingly, when one looks at current fertility variation - e.g. across the country's major states - what one observes to a considerable extent is differences in the timing of fertility decline, more than differences in the impact of these socio-economic variables.

Control over family planning activities has increasingly become the province of individual state governments, rather than of the central government in Delhi. This may not make much difference to the overall tempo of family planning activities in the country. But in some states - perhaps most noticeably Andhra Pradesh - it has meant that politicians have recently instigated fairly aggressive 'target' and 'incentive' driven strategies to promote sterilisation - irrespective of what post-Cairo mainstream opinion may hold. It is hard to gauge how such developments will turn out, but they may play an accelerating role. Particularly important would be improvements in the availability of family planning methods in states like UP and Bihar - because there is little doubt that these states face significant 'supply-side' problems. Of course female education is viewed as a particularly powerful way of increasing fertility control. Between 1991 and 2001 the national literacy rate of females aged seven and above increased from 39 to 54 per cent.

There are many signs that Indian parents are attaching much greater value to the education of their children. This trend too provides support for the idea that fertility in most states will decline at a fairly brisk pace. That said, it should not obscure the fact that especially in the south there are now tens of millions of poor women, with two children, sterilised, and with no education at all. More educated women may reduce their fertility earlier and faster, but after some time less educated women do almost as well. Education affects the timing of the fertility reduction, but its direct impact upon the eventual level of fertility may be negligible.

Especially in those states with relatively low levels of fertility there is an unusually young and extremely concentrated age pattern of fertility. Analysis shows that between the first and second rounds of the NFHS the age location of fertility declined still further and it became even more highly concentrated in almost all the major states. Female sterilisation is the main form of contraception in India. The 1998-99 NFHS found that 34 per cent of currently married women in the country were sterilised, and this method accounted for 71 per cent of total contraceptive prevalence. The median age of female sterilisation was found to be 25.7 years. So - to simply massively - what is suggested is a trend towards a fertility regime in which Indian women continue to start to cohabit at a relatively young age (an age which, admittedly, has probably risen), have two children in fairly quick succession (almost certainly including at least one son), and then get sterilised. Female sterilisation is popular. Past analysts who - quite reasonably - considered that reversible forms of contraception would be required in order to get young Indian women to contracept essentially got the matter wrong.

6.4.1. Regional Dimension

It seems sensible to ask whether there are deep-seated features of Indian society, which may persist to influence fertility behaviour, post the fertility transition. Especially in the later stages of the fertility transition young women increasingly have other avenues for advancement than marriage, having children, and a life spent largely within the domestic family domain. The importance of getting married and having children declines, although of course most women continue to get married and have children. However, given the basic fact of fertility (and to a lesser extent mortality) decline there seems to be no reason why this rationale for below-replacement fertility should not apply in all populations. But there may be variation in certain key social-structural factors - e.g. in the social centrality of marriage - which may affect how readily and quickly below-replacement fertility levels are reached.

Fertility is highest in the four core northern states. And census child woman ratios (CWRs) suggest that until about the last third of the twentieth century fertility in Punjab, Haryana and Gujarat was also comparatively high. Fertility always seems to have been comparatively low in the south; and the southern states experienced fertility declines earlier than the core northern states. Interestingly analysis using district-level CWRs for the period 1951-91 shows fertility decline spreading gradually throughout southern India from an initial 'bridgehead' in the extreme south; this is followed a little later by a second slower emanation of fertility decline from a bridgehead in Punjab/Haryana in the north. Differences in the timing of fertility declines have probably accentuated the current size of the former north/south differential. But the key point is that this differential probably existed prior to the onset of the fertility transition.

The explanation for this demographic contrast is complex. But for present purposes it will suffice to say that northern society tends to place greater stress upon the male line. The main social units are patrilineally related groups of males. Marriages rules are exogamic; 'wife-giving' groups are socially inferior to 'wife-taking' groups; and dowry, which go from the bride's family to that of the groom) is the main marriage transaction. Therefore in the northern kinship system as well as being a fundamental arrangement for the having and rearing of children (especially male heirs) marriage represents a statement of the relationship between different groups. It is central to the structure of the wider society. When women marry they often move over long distances into households where they are strangers. Their levels of personal autonomy are extremely low and son preference is very strong. A daughter will usually require the provision of a dowry.

Producing a son is the chief route for a bride to raise her status. It is often said that son preference in India reflects the Hindu requirement for a son to light the funeral pyre. But this rite can be performed by others than a son, and the highest level of religious merit also requires that a daughter be given in marriage. So the real basis for strong son preference - and daughter neglect - lies in the fundamental arrangements of kinship, inheritance and marriage.

Although some of the more invidious features of the northern kinship system - especially dowry - have increasingly affected parts of south India, the traditional southern system still prevails in places and has strong ramifications. Customary marriage rules in the south tended to be endogenous and women often married men to whom they were related (e.g. cousins or uncles). So the grooms frequently came from familiar households, perhaps in the same village. In this system approximate social equality existed between kin who were related by marriage. And for most of the twentieth century dowry was not very important in most of the south. Accordingly, son preference tends to be significantly weaker, and the birth of a daughter was and is more acceptable. Moreover, because southern women often marry men who they know, spousal relationships tend to be more balanced. After marriage women continue to interact with their parents more frequently than generally applies in the north, and there is less need to re-socialise young brides in their marital homes.

Past international migration has, through mechanisms like the return visits of Indians resident overseas - and their children - had an inordinate effect by helping to spread elements of a so-called western lifestyle. The consequences are very evident among better-off young men and women living in cities like those mentioned above. Increasingly these lifestyle influences have been reflected in the wider media - something, which will happen even more in the years ahead. So south Indian society, in particular, holds out the firm prospect that increasing numbers of young women will carve out independent lives of their own - lives in which marriage and childbearing are less significant. The majority of them will marry, but they and their husbands will be happy with two children or one, even if it is a girl. But irrespective of the child's sex much greater attention will be given to its education. Frequently in occupations like nursing, teaching and service, young women from Kerala can be seen as having been pioneers for some time. And if this state's level of total fertility is not already below replacement, there is nevertheless evidence that the TFR is well below replacement at least for some poor social groups.

The nature of south Indian society is such that in twenty or so years time one can well envisage significant numbers of women in urban areas following their counterparts in South Korea, Thailand and Malaysia where young women are 'staying away from marriage in droves'.

6.5. Conclusion

Forecasting the future is certainly risky and there is always the danger that one will be swept along by the herd. The thrust of this piece has been that a consideration of future fertility trends in India should really be conducted at the state-level. A state-level approach to the formulation of fertility assumptions for population projections leads to a significantly slower rate of fertility decline than does an all-India approach. Total fertility is falling in virtually all of India's states. It is unlikely that in any state the TFR will stagnate for long at a level that is well above replacement. The fertility declines, which are occurring, are ultimately a response to massive and sustained mortality decline. And while it is conceivable that in some states specific interventions - e.g. the instigation of a forceful approach to sterilisation - may accelerate developments, on balance the fertility declines currently underway are probably better considered as having a momentum of their own. That said, India seems set to experience continued social and economic progress, and this should do future fertility decline no harm. South Indian society seems always to have allowed women a little more autonomy in their lives. And southern India - which often seems almost a different country from the north - tends to be socio-economically more advanced and progressive.

References

Natarajan, K.S., *Population Growth in 21st century, Paper presented in the meeting of the Group on Vision 2020.*

Saksena, H. S., "Issues concerning vulnerable groups", *Paper presented in the meeting of the Group on Vision 2020.*

Singh, Padam, "Trends in Fertility, mortality, nutrition and Health indicator", *Paper presented in the meeting of the Group on Vision 2020.*

Srininvasn, K., "Population projections of India and the larger states based on 2001 census results", Paper presented *in the meeting of the Group on Vision 2020.*

Swami Agnivesh, "Child Labour", Paper presented *in the meeting of the Group on Vision 2020.*

7

Causes and Consequences of International Migration

7.1. Introduction

A fundamental characteristic of people is their movement from place to place. The right to move was recognised globally over a half century ago with the adoption of the Universal Declaration of Human Rights. The Declaration states in Article 13 that "Everyone has the right to freedom of movement and residence within the borders of each state" and "Everyone has the right to leave any country, including his own, and to return to his country." International migration can have positive impacts on both the communities of origin and the communities of destination. Migration also has the potential of facilitating the transfer of skills and contributing to cultural enrichment. The vast majority of migrants are making meaningful contributions to their host countries. At the same time, however, international migration entails the loss of human resources for many countries of origin and may give rise to political, economic or social tensions in countries of destination. International migration, with its intricate web of demographic, social, economic and political determinants and consequences, is a topic that has moved to the forefront of national and international agenda. The implementation of national policies to affect levels and patterns of international migration has also intensified, spreading to all regions of the world.

7.2. Measuring International Migration

As the issue of international migration has gained greater importance as a policy agenda item, the demand for international migration information has increased. In particular, international migration statistics and analyses should serve as solid bases for the formulation and the implementation of policies aiming at managing the phenomenon. However, the data that allow the precise estimation of levels and trends of international population movements and the investigation of its causes and consequences are far from complete. International monitoring and reporting initiatives are seriously hindered by data availability, quality, and comparability, thus calling for improved coordination of data-gathering activities among those who are concerned with global estimates of international migration.

Despite the data on international migration are scarce, statistical sources that can potentially produce information relevant to international migration are quite diverse. Possibly, the sense of scarcity partly stems from the limited access to these data. Many existing data-collecting systems are set up to answer the demands of different administrative objectives, and therefore, not necessarily valued as sources of information to measure the volume of international migration. Dissemination of information generated by those systems has been often limited, or has been slow if it is ever released. Hence, one of the fundamental challenges for data-compilation at international level is the identification of appropriate data sources and timely access to the data.

There is no single source of data that can reflect the growing complexity of the international population movements. A variety of sources produce different types of migration statistics, with its own strengths and limitations. National population registers, if a country maintains the system, can be a valuable source of data on both inflows and outflows of citizens. However, the identification of international migrants is subject to the rules concerning inscription in or de-registration from the register. Moreover, when individuals do not comply strictly with the rules, the true extend of population mobility tends to be understated. Similar biases affect the data derived from registers of foreigners. While registers of foreigners may capture the influx of foreigners granted the permission to reside in a country, the coverage of those leaving the country is likely to be less complete, because of their reluctance to report the departure.

7.2.1. Labour Migration

Over the past three decades, policies in the area of labour migration have developed along four major paths: growing restrictiveness and selectiveness in the admission of labour migrants in developed countries; a significant increase in the number of countries, particularly developing countries, that have become host to foreign workers; the rising recognition that the rights of migrant workers and their families need to be protected and; the adoption of regional agreements on the free movement of persons.

The nature, direction and magnitude of labour migration have clearly been influenced by economic and political changes taking place in the world. The economic turmoil that followed the oil shocks of the 1970s led many governments to adopt measures that put an end to the relatively relaxed immigration controls that had characterised the post-war period. The change in policy resulted in a major decline in the number of migrant workers admitted in countries with developed market economies. In most of the labour-importing countries of Western and Northern Europe, the recruitment of regular migrant labour practically ceased. With a view to protecting the domestic labour markets in the context of rapidly growing unemployment, many Governments also implemented repatriation programmes that provided incentives for migrant workers to return to their home country. These programmes had limited success, although the overall number of, at least temporary returnees, was on the order of several hundred thousand.

The recruitment of foreign labour on the basis of skills has had a significant influence on the origin and nature of overall migration flows. Under the current preference system, newly arrived immigrants in the United States are more likely to come from Asia and Europe, while in Canada and Australia, the numerical weight attached to factors such as education, training, occupation, and language skills has reduced the proportion of immigrants dependent on family relationships.

Migration provisions for skilled workers differ significantly from provisions for other types of migration prevailing in countries of permanent settlement and labour importing developed countries. In settlement countries, skilled workers are only granted temporary residence and are, therefore, not put on a permanent immigration track. In contrast, in labour importing developed countries, skilled workers are often contracted for a period that may significantly exceed the length of time granted for other types of work. In addition, some countries, such as the United Kingdom are taking steps towards allowing highly skilled persons to seek entry without having a prior offer of employment.

A number of developed countries, including the EU as a whole, have taken steps towards the formulation of such agreements. Concern has also been raised at the potential impact of such agreements for sending countries in terms of brain-drain issues, particularly in the health and education sectors. A second major policy development in the area of labour migration has been the significant increase in the number of countries, particularly developing countries that have become host to foreign workers.

The small size of the populations, the low female labour force participation rates, the low status of manual labour and a reluctance to work in the private sector made it very difficult to alleviate the labour shortages created by the economic boom without importing foreign workers. Therefore, the oil-producing countries of the Gulf region became the main destination for migrant workers from Asia.

Replacement migration refers to the international migration that is needed to offset declines in the size of population and declines in the population of working age, as well as to compensate for the overall ageing of population. One of the major findings of the study was that the level of migration needed to offset population ageing is extremely high and entails vastly more immigration than has occurred in the past.

7.2.2. Immigration of Family Members

Since the 1980s, family reunification has become a major source of immigration in a significant number of countries, particularly in Europe. In OECD countries as a whole, migration for family reunification accounts for the largest share of migrant intake. To a large extent, the significance of migration for family reunification is a direct consequence of the restrictions imposed on labour migration in the mid-1970s. Family reunion has become the main legal means of migration, apart from asylum. In Western

Europe, the surge in migration for family reunification took Governments by surprise. Many Governments wanted to implement a zero migration policy and hoped that by halting the recruitment of labour migrants this would be achieved. For many years, this attitude entailed an official denial of the existence of any major migration flow in most Western European countries.

As no international instrument universally establishes family reunification as a right, immigration for family reunification largely exists as a privilege granted by national authorities to the individual, based on both the right to family life and the right to travel. Implementation of family reunification is, therefore, discretionary, although international norms and human rights agreements have placed some moral and political constraints on the State. Beside human rights considerations, countries of permanent immigration have traditionally valued family reunification as being conducive to integration, and therefore have facilitated reunification. In contrast, in labour-importing countries, much of the debate has focused on the cost of providing migrants' dependents with health, education and welfare benefits.

In all countries, family members who are known to constitute a threat to public order or national security are not admitted through family reunification. It is, however, difficult to determine the practice and the thoroughness of verification. A few countries ask for documentary evidence of absence of criminal record, while others only check for selected offences. There has been discussion of whether a different set of rules should apply to refugees who cannot provide the necessary document or may have been sentenced under criminal law. In some countries, family members are not eligible if they have medical conditions that endanger public health. At the end of the 1980s, concern with the spread of the HIV/AIDS virus led some countries to deny access to migrants suspected of being infected.

7.2.3. Refugees and Asylum Seekers

Whereas asylum and migration were long viewed as separate issues by Governments, asylum policies are now at the core of the discussions on migration in many parts of world. This major change in perspective has been triggered by the surge in the number of refugees during thc 1980s and early 1990s, a trend that ran contrary to the pursuit of restrictive migration policies by an increasing number of Governments. The international asylum regime that had prevailed from the early 1950s through the late 1990s eventually challenged the States' prerogative to decide on the admission of foreigners, an issue that was brought to the public attention by the extensive media coverage of refugees and significantly contributed to the politicisation of migration.

The implicit assumption of such policies is that most asylum seekers are in fact economic migrants. The measures taken include visa requirements, sanctions against carriers, in-country processing and the adoption of the "safe country" principle under which an asylum-seeker can be denied access to national asylum procedures and sent back to a safe third country, if they had travelled through such country prior to applying for asylum. In addition, many countries now resort to rapid asylum procedures for "manifestly unfounded applications" and enforce removal decisions concerning rejectees, often by way of detention so as to facilitate deportation. Stricter control during the processing of applications has been in effect, ranging from fingerprinting to quasi house arrest in reception facilities.

7.2.4. Undocumented Migration

The magnitude of undocumented migration, by its very nature, remains difficult to quantify. The exact dimension of the undocumented migration phenomenon is therefore difficult to define. Nevertheless, it is widely believed that undocumented migration has been on the rise since the mid-1970s, particularly in developed countries. All other things being equal, this upward trend in undocumented migration has been the outcome of both increasingly restrictive admission policies in receiving countries and the fact that a large number of countries have relaxed emigration/exit controls following the end of the Cold War. A relatively new and salient dimension of undocumented migration is that of trafficking.

Trafficking ranges from small-scale operators who provide transport across a border to, increasingly, international criminal networks that provide an entire range of services, including bogus documentation, transportation and assistance in crossing borders, places for transit and residence in receiving countries and illegal employment. In a context of growing anti-immigrant feelings in receiving countries and politicisation of migration, most Governments have repeatedly placed the clamping down on smuggling at the top of the migration policy agenda. Measures adopted to combat undocumented migration include information campaigns, visa requirements, carrier sanctions, document and border controls and sanctions against undocumented foreigners, smugglers and employers.

7.3. International Migration and Development

International migration has been receiving increasing attention at the policy level, as a global phenomenon involving a growing number of countries. In the mid-1970s international migration was a topic of secondary concern for many Governments; their intervention was mostly confined to the administrative regulation of national borders. Over the past decades, the number of Governments adopting measures to control these flows has increased.

Several Governments also considered that the complex issues of international migration could be most productively addressed through regional negotiations, so that conditions particular to the region can be factored into concrete policy responses. The five Governments that expressed only partial support for the convening of a conference felt that more work was necessary to clarify and define its objectives. They generally considered that regional or bilateral negotiations were more likely to lead to meaningful ways of dealing with the issue of international migration, as did some of the Governments that did not favour the holding of a conference.

7.3.1. Government Views and Policies on Immigration

Governments assessment of the current level of overall immigration into the country. It is divided into three categories: too low; satisfactory; too high. Policy refers to Government policies towards the current level of immigration for permanent settlement. It is divided into four categories: to raise the level of immigration; to maintain the level of immigration; to lower the level of immigration; and no intervention. The major sources of information used to document Governments' international migration views and policies may be classified into four broad types. The first type of information comprises official Government responses to the United Nations Population Inquiry Among Governments, of which eight rounds were conducted between 1963 and 1998. The second type of information consists of documents and statements issued by Governments, including laws, regulations and bi- and multi-lateral agreements. The third type of information comprises materials prepared by international organisations, such as regional commissions, funds, programmes and agencies of the United Nations system, as well as other intergovernmental organisations. The fourth type of information consists of non-governmental materials, including clippings from the world press, articles in academic journals, proceedings of conferences and seminars, reports prepared by research centres and non-governmental organisations, as well as correspondence and personal communications with experts.

The change in the patterns of international migration from and within the Asia-Pacific region took place at a time when economic growth was taking off in the region, thereby hinting at the links between migration and social change, and particularly between migration and development. Asia used to be a region marked by poverty and international migration, then was mostly directed to the West.

The gulf between these newly industrialised countries and the less developing countries added another dimension to the political, cultural, social and demographic diversities in Asia. Economic growth in the NICs opened educational and occupational opportunities for their nationals, leaving some sectors in need of workers willing to take up low-end jobs. Gaps in living standards and disparities in capital and labour supply and labour demand contributed to the conditions that set the stage for labour migration within the region.

Outside of the migration literature, the link between increasing labour migration and the East Asian economic miracle is not that appreciated. Receiving Governments do not readily acknowledge the role of labour migration in the development of their societies. The denial or the refusal to allow the importation of migrant workers by some receiving countries, however, did not stop labour migration from taking place. During the period of high economic growth, migrant workers were tolerated, especially since they took jobs shunned by local workers.

In contrast, countries of origin acknowledge the contributions of international migration, citing such benefits as providing a safety net for unemployment, the role of remittances in generating foreign exchange and technology transfer/skills acquisition. For these reasons, some countries of origin consider migration in their development plans. Analysts and observers note that Asia will have to brace for a different economic environment in the twenty-first century. Globalisation, information technology and democratisation are changing the world Asia faces in the new century. Prospects for growth in other parts of the region seem bleak since the supply of capital to export industries—an important factor in the rise of second-tier NICs—has dwindled considerably. The crisis exposed the weaknesses and vulnerabilities in Asian economies, particularly the lack of effective social safety nets.

7.4. Asia-Pacific Migration System

Considering the diversity of the region and the migration systems that have developed therein, a summary of international labour migration trends is presented by sub-region. The review begins with the South Asia-West Asia connections. Embarking on an industrialisation project fuelled by oil revenues, the Gulf countries tapped countries in South Asia and later, South-East Asia, to meet their huge labour requirements. In the 1980s, NIC-hood spread from Japan to other countries in East and South-East Asia. Coinciding with the slowdown in the demand for workers in the Gulf countries, these two regions provided alternative destinations for migrant workers. In North and Central Asia, political changes rather than economic changes augured international migrations in the 1990s. Finally, in Oceania, Australia and New Zealand increasingly attracted Asian immigrants, in addition to being the focal points of immigration from the Pacific islands.

The migration of the less skilled, but it should be mentioned that movements of the highly skilled and professionals are also taking place as are other types of temporary migration. Permanent emigration to traditional countries of settlement also continues, with Asia figuring as a major region of origin of migrants. Refugee migrations are almost a fixture in the region, with new conflict zones emerging as soon as solutions to old conflicts have been reached. These different types of migration—labour migration, the migration of the highly skilled and professionals, permanent migration and refugee migration—proceed either through regular or irregular channels.

7.4.1. South Asia and West Asia

Bangladesh, India and Pakistan had supplied the Middle East with workers since the 1970s. A relative latecomer to the Gulf countries, Sri Lanka pursued the export of domestic helpers, the only country in South Asia where women comprise the great majority of irregular migration refers to departure from the rules and norms of the migration regime of a country of origin, transit or destination while trafficking is a more violent and abusive form of irregular migration. As defined in the United Nations Protocol to Prevent, Suppress and Punish Trafficking in Persons, Especially Women and Children, trafficking in persons shall mean the "recruitment, transportation, transfer, harbouring or receipt of persons, by means of the threat or use of force or other forms of coercion, of abduction, of fraud, of deception, of the abuse of power or of a position of vulnerability or of the giving or receiving of payments or benefits to achieve the consent of a person having control over another person, for the purpose of exploitation. Exploitation shall include, at a minimum, the exploitation of the prostitution of others or other forms of sexual exploitation, forced labour or services, slavery or practices similar to slavery, servitude or the removal of organs."

The Government is active in promoting labour migration in the case of Bangladesh, Pakistan and Sri Lanka. In these three countries, State agencies are involved in promoting labour export, monitoring the conditions of their workers abroad and promoting the welfare of migrants and their families. The reliance of South Asian countries on the Gulf labour market renders them vulnerable to changes in the latter. Although the de-stabilising impacts of the 1991 Gulf War turned out to be temporary, the experience highlighted the precariousness of relying on a single destination. Changes in the labour demand in the Gulf countries are forthcoming, especially with their goal of nationalising their work force.

South Asian countries will have to invest in human resource development programmes in order to be competitive. Also, in the long term, they will have to tap other destinations as the Gulf countries move to reduce their dependence on foreign workers. Intra-regional migration also takes place in South Asia, but such flows tend to be either forced migration or irregular migration. Almost all of the South Asian countries are either origin or receiving countries for refugees and asylum seekers, the internally displaced and other persons of concern.

The Islamic Revolution in 1979 severely strained relations between the Islamic Republic of Iran and the Western powers. Last year, the drought contributed to refugee movements from Afghanistan. The withdrawal of Soviet forces in 1989 did not put an end to refugee migration from Afghanistan. Conflicts between the Taliban and rival forces created a resurgence of refugee migration in the 1990s. India and Pakistan are confronted with the problem of irregular migration involving Bangladeshis. India has attempted to solve the problem through occasional crackdowns, repatriation and the construction of a border fence. Pakistan, however, plans on holding a registration exercise to better monitor the situation. In recent years, trafficking in women and children has been reported from poverty-stricken areas of Bangladesh and Nepal to India (mostly for prostitution); and the trafficking of young boys from Bangladesh, Pakistan and India to be used as camel jockeys in the Middle East. Recognition of the problem and the need to address it has led to the drawing up of a draft convention in 1997.

7.4.2. East Asia

East Asian destinations admit skilled workers and professionals, but are less welcoming of less skilled workers. Hong Kong, China allows for the admission of less skilled workers through its labour supplementation scheme, the entry route for construction workers and domestic helpers. The continuing demand for foreign domestic helpers since the 1970s has made Hong Kong, China one of the major destinations of women migrants.

Japan postponed the importation of foreign workers through relocation and upgrading. The clamour to import workers came from small- and medium-sized firms, which could not afford the two other options. Then and now, Japan has maintained a policy of not accepting less skilled workers. Irregular migrant workers filled the shortfall. Japan's discovery of the migrant presence prompted it to revise its immigration law in 1990, but not the policy about unskilled workers. The sluggish economy in the 1990s dampened the demand for unskilled workers. In 2000, Japan toughened its policies against overstayers. Japan accepts entertainers, who are classified under the skilled and professional category. The two major source countries of entertainers are the Philippines and Thailand. While there has been a notable decline in the number of irregular migrants in the country, the demand for entertainers has been stable, even through the 1997-1998 crisis. Aside from the legal route, entertainers are brought in through irregular channels, including trafficking in women. Although Japan is not a country of immigration, some permanent settlement is taking place via marriages between Japanese nationals and foreigners. International marriages in Japan were mostly between Japanese women and foreign men, until 1975, when more and more Japanese men married women from other Asian countries. The longterm settlement and community formation of some groups in Japan challenge the notion of a homogeneous Japanese society.

Taiwan Province of China crafted a migration policy that recognises the need for less skilled workers in the construction, manufacturing and household sectors. To ensure that migrant workers do not stay, migrant workers can only work in Taiwan Province of China for a maximum of three years, without any extension or renewal thereafter. Taiwan Province of China was not as badly affected during the 1997-1998 crisis, but it did not remain immune to economic vagaries. The United States-led economic slowdown which started last year, particularly the slump in the demand for electronic goods, has Taiwan Province of China's economy floundering.

China encourages labour export as a means to reduce unemployment pressures, but it has figured more in international migration because of the much-publicised cases of smuggling of Chinese to other countries in East Asia and to distant countries in North America and Europe. Aside from exorbitant fees, migrants could be subjected to various forms of risks, abuses and violence during passage or continued subjection once they arrive at the destination. Although China is not (yet) a major country of origin of migrant workers, its 824-million-strong working age population, poses stiff competition for other labour exporters. Also, the competition China could wage in terms of offering the lowest production costs could be an alternative to importing labour. Both scenarios have implications for narrowing the migration opportunities of other countries of origin in the region.

7.4.3. Southeast Asia

Southeast Asia is a vibrant mix of countries of destination, countries that send and receive workers and countries of origin. Among the countries of destination, Singapore had a migration framework before large numbers of foreign workers arrived in the city-State. It acknowledged that it needs less skilled labour, but it is also bent on reducing its dependence on foreign labour. Singapore has managed labour migration based on a system of quotas and levies. It is actively seeking foreign talent, which it sees as essential to maintain its competitiveness. Malaysia and Thailand evolved policies on labour migration when large numbers of migrant workers were already present in their labour markets. Both countries underwent industrial transformation during the 1980s and the early 1990s, thanks to export-led industrialisation and the infusion of foreign direct investment. This resulted in an increasing share of manufacturing and services in GDP and employment.

High economic growth and high employment growth required workers, which their labour markets could not provide. This was particularly problematic for Malaysia, given its small population. In both countries, the agriculture sector was the first to experience labour shortage, and later on this spread to the manufacturing sector as well. Migrant workers from neighbouring countries filled the need for workers in the agriculture, service and construction sectors. Their proximity to neighbouring low-wage countries greatly facilitated the unauthorised movement of labour. Their numbers swelled to problematic proportions. Several regularisation/amnesty exercises were carried out and they also resorted to crackdowns, border controls, sanctions on immigration violators and repatriation.

Irregular migration did not abate despite these measures. Thailand recently admitted that these measures had not been effective and has decided to adopt a work permit system. Employers and irregular migrant workers were given until 29 September 2001 to register foreign workers. The change was expected to enable the Government to monitor migrant workers in the country and provide better protection to workers. Malaysia, however, will have to design a more consistent, long-term migration policy that is linked to an economic restructuring programme in a planned effort to phase out labour importation

Most of it is regular migration. The other magnet is Sabah, which is grappling with irregular migration from the Philippines and Indonesia. The various estimates of the foreign population in Sabah reflect the difficulty of ascertaining their number.

The active participation of the Government in labour export is most evident in the case of the Philippines and Indonesia. Among the countries of origin in Asia, the Philippines sends the largest number of workers abroad, workers of varying skill levels, and to more destinations the world over. By contrast, labour migration from Indonesia is mostly unskilled and is directed mainly to neighbouring Malaysia and Saudi Arabia, and more recently, Hong Kong, China and Taiwan Province of China. Since the 1990s, women make up the majority of migrant workers legally deployed from the Philippines and Indonesia, most of whom work as domestic helpers. The Philippine Government initially focused on marketing its workers, but it later included programmes and services promoting the welfare and protection of migrants. These programmes and initiatives, covering pre-migration, on-site and return and re-integration issues, serve as examples of good practices for consideration by other countries of origin.

Economic growth in the 1990s halted labour migration from Thailand, but it was encouraged by the Government when the crisis hit in 1997. Other Asian countries are the major destinations of Thai workers, and in Taiwan Province of China, Thais have been the largest group since the 1990s. Malaysia is also a country of origin, but Malaysians have not migrated in large numbers to distant destinations. Malaysians migrate to work in Singapore.

The break-up of the Soviet Union loosened border control, and the CEE/CIS became a destination as well as a transit point for immigrants seeking entry to Western Europe. There is paucity of data on migration and many population movements are not captured. Some 700,000 to 1.5 million persons are estimated to be working in the CIS without work permits. There are also indications that the region is being used as a transit point for irregular migration, including the trafficking of women from Central and Eastern Europe.

According to a United States report, in 1997 some 175,000 women and girls from CEE and CIS were trafficked, one fourth of all women trafficked worldwide.

7.4.4. Pacific

Australia and New Zealand are the only countries in the Asia-Pacific region that offer the possibility for permanent immigration. Asia became the top source region of immigrants to these two countries with the dismantling of migration policies that traditionally favoured Europeans in the 1970s and in 1986. Immigration criteria in both countries are based on family, skills and humanitarian considerations. Immigrants with capital can also qualify under business investment programmes. In Australia, amendments were introduced in 1996 to make the process more selective; hence skills and English language proficiency were emphasised and access to welfare support was limited. New Zealand also implemented more selective measures in 1995 after immigration had increased in the 1990s, particularly from "non-traditional" sources.

7.4.5. Initiating and Sustaining International Migration

7.4.5.1. Factors initiate migration

Theorising about migration (specifically labour migration) has focused on the questions of why migration occurs and why it continues. For the longest time, the field has been dominated by neoclassical economics (also called equilibrium theory)—push-pull factors and rational choice theory. Other perspectives have developed which provide competing explanations regarding migration: the new economics of labour migration, segmented labour market theory and world systems theory were advanced to answer the first question, and the social capital theory and cumulative causation look into the continuation of migration. Each of these perspectives illuminates specific aspects of migration, but each one by itself cannot provide a sufficient explanation of the causes of migration.

Neoclassical economics informs much of the research looking into the causes of migration. Income and wage differentials are widely accepted as a principal underlying cause of international migration in the Asia-Pacific region and are the starting point of many descriptive studies. The limitations of neoclassical economics are also evident in the region: as elsewhere, the poorest countries, the poorest families and the poorest individuals are not the ones most likely to migrate. The new economics of migration holds that migration is a household rather than an individual-level decision. It recognises that families and households in developing countries are vulnerable not just to failures in the labour market but in other markets as well.

The segmented labour market theory links migration with the structural changes evolving in industrial societies. According to this perspective, migration is inevitable, resulting from the built-in demand for migrant workers in the secondary labour market of industrial societies. Few studies have been undertaken to test the propositions of segmented labour market theory in the region. However, indirect evidence—migration trends vis-à-vis industrialisation in the region—suggests that migration is structural and demand-driven. The preceding discussion noted that virtually all labour importing countries have a demand for less skilled workers (although the official policies of some countries do not recognise this). Usually this demand comes from small- and medium-sized firms, which, unlike large firms, are not in a position to go the road of high technology or to relocate overseas. In the process, the labour market bifurcates into the primary sector, which offers jobs fetching high wages and tenure, and the secondary sector, which offers low-end jobs, low wages and no security. Jobs in the primary sector attract local workers while the secondary labour market becomes the niche for migrant workers.

Women's migration and their concentration in domestic services and entertainment suggest that the labour market is not only segmented but also gendered. Like other unskilled work, the migration of female domestic helpers and entertainers is demand-driven, with a void left by local women when they take up productive work. Without significant changes in the organisation of reproductive work—the work that is needed to support social life that is usually assumed by women—importing women migrants is one strategy to address the shortage. Thus, in the process of structural change, reproductive work becomes part of the 3D jobs that are passed on to migrant workers. The cheaper costs and flexibility of migrant labour, i.e., importing and repatriating workers as the economic situation warrants, are advantages that markets cannot do without. In the case of women migrant workers, the necessity of reproductive work in sustaining social life suggests a constant demand for such workers. Reproductive work is also work that requires the presence of a caregiver; hence, it cannot be fully replaced by automation or relocated. Indeed, as the experience during the crisis bears out, domestic helpers and entertainers were hardly affected by lay-offs or repatriation.

The region's experience during the 1997-1998 crisis also confirms the built-in demand for migrant labour in industrialised societies. The receiving countries—Malaysia, Thailand and the Republic of Korea—carried out repatriation programmes in the hope that unemployed local workers will move into the jobs vacated by migrant workers. The repatriation programmes took place and border control and other measures helped to keep out illegal entrants. However, even during a period of unemployment, local workers did not take up the jobs vacated by migrants, and some sectors experienced labour shortages. They had to modify or postpone their repatriation plans owing to labour shortages in the plantation sector in Malaysia and in the rice mill and fishing industries in Thailand. This experience underscored the fact that migrant workers and local workers do not compete with each other, i.e., they work in different sectors. Migrant workers thus complement rather than substitute for local workers.

Globalisation has conflicting tendencies and contradictions. Migration is one area where the promise of a borderless world flounders. While Governments may be willing to liberalise flows of trade or capital, they are more likely to exert control on the flows of people. However, other consequences or associated processes of globalisation could mean more migration because of new migration pressures or the facilitative role played by transnational communities and networks and cheaper and faster transportation. The globalisation of the capitalist economy began in the sixteenth century via colonisation and it is in this sense that globalisation is not a new phenomenon. The new aspects of globalisation in this era are new markets, new tools, new actors and new rules. Although current usage of the term emphasises the economic aspects, globalisation also has technological, cultural and political aspects.

7.4.5.2. Factors sustain migration

The possibility that migration will come to an end is predicted in neoclassical economics: e.g., when wage differentials disappear, or as trade theory indicates, by substituting the movement of goods with the movement of labour. The experience of several East Asian countries suggests that their transition from labour-exporting to labour importing countries proceeded after reaching a certain level of economic development. Adopting an eclectic approach to turning points in migration, Fong emphasises that a country's net migration position evolves as it develops and as it is influenced by economic, policy and institutional factors.

The path and the time it takes a country to turn into a labour-receiving country vary greatly. Insights from social capital theory and cumulative causation help to explain why labour migration continues in the face of restrictive migration policies in receiving countries and regulation in countries of origin. These two perspectives recognise that migration is also a social process, drawing attention to the role of informal and formal institutions in increasing migration.

Migrant networks (personal and social networks of migrants) and migrant institutions (migrant organisations and the migration industry) promote further migration. Migrant networks facilitate migration by linking migrants and non-migrants. Information, resources and promise of assistance and support from migrant kin and friends reduce the risks of migration and increase the possibility for migration. Over time, migrant institutions emerge, providing institutional responses to the challenges and opportunities of migration.

7.4.6. Consequences of International Migration

The impacts of international migration have been the subject of much speculation, but research in this area is uneven and generally inconclusive. In the countries of destination, migrants are generally regarded negatively or ignored. Migrants have been blamed for or are feared to cause various problems: rise in crime, spread of diseases, taking away jobs from locals or driving down the wages of local workers. In the case of foreign domestic helpers, their influence on the young has been a cause for concern. The media's tendency to focus on migrants arrested for migration violations or problems they encountered add to the perception of migration as a problem-ridden issue.

Among the countries in the Asia-Pacific region, Australia is an exception because of the availability of migration data, an important resource for generating research-based information. Research in Australia reveals that immigration has had a positive impact on Australian society. The findings confirmed that Australia's economy and social cohesion have not been adversely affected by immigration. The issue of migration impacts has received considerable attention in the countries of origin.

The demand for foreign workers will continue, despite the goal of countries of destination to phase out their dependence on foreign workers. The experience of the now developed countries supports the dual labour market theory's proposition of the necessity of importing workers to perform less skilled jobs. What the dual labour market theory did not anticipate is the emergence of a demand for highly skilled and professional migrants as well, which arises as economies continue the shift from manufacturing to the tertiary sector.

International labour migration is one strategy to meet shortages in the skilled labour market, which is critical to support growth and to be competitive. For this reason, the welcome mat is spread out generously to the highly skilled. As mentioned earlier, countries of destination in Asia are open to the highly skilled and professionals. Some countries have designed programmes to attract these kinds of migrants. They are sought out and are provided with benefits and incentives that are not extended to less skilled migrants. Aside from the gains to receiving countries, there are social development gains for the countries of origin and the migrants as well. The former could generate more remittances and there is also the possibility of technology transfer and skills formation, which are not realisable in less skilled migration. For individual migrants, aside from higher wages, this kind of migration could promote career advancement. They can also be assured of better protection and they can have a family life as well. There will be a continuing demand for less skilled migrants, but the prospects for social development are more uneven. In the countries of destination, employers and consumers may benefit from this arrangement, but the less educated and older sectors of the population could be displaced or vulnerable to low wages.

The protection of less skilled workers will become even more crucial in the emerging environment. Observers have noted the increasing costs of labour migration, which could reduce the returns of investment of migrants and their families. Brokers and intermediaries, both legal and illegal entities, have become important players in facilitating labour migration. In the competition for jobs in a limited and restricted international labour market, the costs are passed on to migrants. To meet these obligations, migrants get into debt, which requires them to work abroad longer in order to recoup their investments. This affects both legal and irregular migrants, although the latter tend to be more vulnerable. This is one aspect of labour migration which requires the cooperation of the origin and destination countries. Efforts on the part of countries of origin to monitor or regulate placement and recruitment agencies should be matched by efforts of destination countries to monitor employment agencies and employers.

7.4.7. Threat of Irregular Migration

Irregular migration in Asia is not likely to decline. As in regular migration, those involved in irregular migration have also established networks and migrant institutions across transnational spaces, thereby facilitating further flows. Owing to their clandestine nature, such institutions are beyond the reach of government regulations and develop a life of their own. Irregular migration is not only expensive but it also exacts other costs on migrants—a precarious existence as an irregular migrant, lack of access to basic services and no means of redress for grievances, among others. Irregular migration also seriously compromises the integrity of the asylum process and thereby jeopardises the asylum chances of bona fide refugees.

Victims of trafficking are victimised many times over: being deceived, sold or abducted; being used for sexual exploitation, forced labour or domestic servitude or being forced into marriage; confinement; exposure to life-threatening conditions, including STDs and HIV/AIDS; or abuse at the hands of the authorities. The various discussions on the issue converge on the following basic approaches: to prevent it from happening through education; to protect victims of trafficking; to prosecute traffickers; and to provide assistance and services for the rehabilitation of victims of trafficking. Migration pressures are greater for the poor, but as documented by various studies, the very poor cannot migrate because of lack of resources. Traffickers are aware of this and capitalise on the economic vulnerability of the poor to advance their pecuniary interests in the trade of people.

7.5. Women and International Migration

Women often migrate officially as dependent family members of other migrants or to marry someone in another country. Female migrants are, however, increasingly part of flows of migrant workers, moving on their own to become the principal wage earners for their families. Most migrant women move voluntarily, but women and girls are also forced migrants leaving their countries in order to flee conflict, persecution, environmental degradation, natural disasters or other situations that affect their security, livelihood or habitat. As a key organising principle of society, gender is central to any discussion of the causes and consequences of international migration, including the process of decision-making involved and the mechanisms leading to migration. Previous approaches to documenting and understanding international migration have often disregarded the migration of women. Analytical frameworks either ignored the participation of women in international migration and their contributions or assumed that the causes and consequences of international migration were similar for migrant women and migrant men, thus avoiding an investigation of how migration and its outcomes differ by sex.

It is important to understand the causes and consequences of international migration from a gender perspective because hierarchical social relations related to gender shape the migration experiences of migrants, whether male or female. Understanding whether migration occurs because of gender inequality or whether migration itself helps to perpetuate gender disparities is important to guide the formulation of policy and measures to address the specific needs of women who migrate.

The participation of women in migration depends on the social roles of women, their autonomy and capacity to make decisions, their access to resources, and the existing gender stratification in countries of origin and destination. Gender inequality can be a powerful factor leading to migration when women have economic, political and social expectations that cannot be realised in the country of origin. As with any migrant, the migration outcomes for women vary depending on whether their movement is voluntary or forced, and on whether their presence in the receiving country is legal or not.

For both women and men, the economic and political context of the country of origin conditions how migration decisions are made and how migration occurs. When practices or policies in the country of origin discriminate against women by, for instance, limiting their access to resources or educational opportunities, or by hindering their political participation, the capacity of women to participate fully in society and contribute to it is reduced. These limitations also affect the potential of women to migrate and determine whether women can migrate autonomously or not. Gender relations within the family determine who migrates on their own, women or men. Gender norms about the inappropriateness of women migrating autonomously, the constraining effects of their traditional family roles, women's lack of social and economic independence, all hinder women's participation in international migration. The migration of women is also limited by their lack of connections to social networks in the country of destination that could provide information and resources to make the move possible.

Women migrate to work abroad in response to gender-specific labour demand in countries of destination that reflects existing values, norms, stereotypes and hierarchies based on gender. Thus, although laws regarding the admission of migrant workers are generally gender neutral, the demand for domestic workers, nurses, and entertainers focuses on the recruitment of migrant women. Moreover, in countries of origin as well, female labour supply is the result of gender norms and stereotypes that gear women to certain traditionally female occupations. Recruitment intermediaries, whether private or official, also contribute to reinforce gender segregation in the labour market. In addition, expectations about reciprocity within the family in countries of origin may favour the migration of women if daughters are seen as more likely to remit consistently and to undertake the responsibility of helping the family left behind. Migration is related to the level of empowerment of women, with migration levels among women being higher when female earning potential is more highly valued in the country of origin and women have access to local employment and income-generating opportunities. However, access to such opportunities may dampen the need or desire for migration.

Migration affects not only the migrants themselves but also their family members even if they remain in the country origin. Gender relations and gender hierarchies in both sending and receiving countries determine the gender-specific impact of migration. Women remaining behind when their male relatives (husbands or parents) migrate may find themselves co-residing with other male relatives who may restrict their activities outside the home. In many instances, women left behind in the country of origin must undertake income generating activities to compensate for the income lost by the departure of their male relatives if the latter do not send remittances on a regular basis. Adding financial responsibilities to the other responsibilities that women have, such as child-rearing, can lead to stress but can also provide women the opportunity of gaining autonomy and experience in decision-making.

In the societies of destination, gender relations and hierarchies as well as policies or practices leading to gender inequities condition the effects of migration for migrant women. The legal status of migrant women, the gender norms implicit in admission regulations and general attitudes to migrants are also important factors influencing the subsequent experiences of migrant women and the impact of their migration on countries of destination. Conventions, laws and practices governing the rights of women and migrants in receiving countries affect migrant women. Women who are recruited as domestic workers or those who are unauthorised workers in the country of destination are particularly vulnerable. Depending on the receiving country, they may have no protection or recourse in case of abuse. Migrant women are also affected by gender inequality in the society of destination. Labour market segmentation based on gender and the segregation of women in traditionally female occupations (nursing, secretarial work, garment industry work, etc.) mean that migrant women are often paid less that migrant men who are concentrated in higher-paying occupations. Thus earning inequality between migrant women and migrant men persists in countries of destination. When migrants start small businesses in the country of destination, female family members may work without remuneration in response to norms and practices that undervalue their contributions.

Nonetheless, when women become migrant workers or participate in the labour market of the receiving society, they tend to gain independence and autonomy, leading to a change in gender relations within their families. Gains of that nature at the household level may, however, do not necessarily extend to other spheres of a woman's life, such as the place of employment or within her ethnic community at large.

Migrant women display considerable agency. They contribute to the economic development of their countries of destination through their competencies and skills, and to that of their countries of origin through their remittances and their increased experience when they return to those countries. Often, migrant women help other family members to migrate by paying for the costs of the move. As migrants, women are sources of remittances that may be used to improve the well being of other family members and foster economic growth. In countries of destination, migrant women work to improve their own and their family's standards of living, and they often press for changed gender relations within their families. In many countries, they also form and participate in non-governmental organisations that lobby for gender equality. Upon return to the countries of origin, migrant women may disseminate the importance of rights and opportunities for women.

Refugee women and girls or those who are displaced are particularly vulnerable when they find themselves in situations where their security cannot be ensured and where they may be subject to sexual violence or exploitation. Providing women and children who are refugees or displaced access to food and other essential items is critical, as is their participation in decisions regarding their future and that of their families. The trafficking of women and girls for prostitution and forced labour is one of the fastest growing areas of international criminal activity. Women who are trafficked are the most vulnerable of all migrants as the process of trafficking involves exploitation, coercion and the abuse of power. Trafficking builds on existing gender inequalities. Trafficked women frequently originate from regions where there are few employment opportunities for women and where women are dependent on others and lack access to resources to change their situation. Trafficked women and girls often believe they will work in legitimate occupations but find themselves trapped into forced prostitution, marriage, domestic work, sweatshops and other forms of exploitation that are similar to slavery. Strategies need to be developed to protect and empower women in these situations. Actions to prevent trafficking include the dissemination of information on the modes used by traffickers to attract and entrap women, the dangers involved and the legal channels open for migration, as well as the provision of better employment opportunities in the country of origin.

A number of international instruments outline the human rights of migrants. Yet many national laws regulating the admission and stay of international migrants include provisions that negatively impact the human rights of migrant women. For instance, laws may include provisions that bar female migrants from being accompanied by their husbands and children or that make it difficult for migrant women to achieve family reunification. In addition, because of the types of occupations that migrant women are concentrated in, they may not receive adequate legal protection under labour laws, especially if they work as domestic workers. Increased understanding of the situation of migrant women should provide the basis for the formulation of policies and programmes that promote their equality with migrant men and that safeguard their well-being.

7.6. Conclusion

Enhance international cooperation, including burden-sharing, and coordination of humanitarian assistance to countries affected by natural disasters and other humanitarian emergencies and post-conflict situations in ways that will be supportive of recovery and long-term development. Create and improve conditions to allow for the voluntary repatriation of refugees in safety and dignity to their countries of origin, and the voluntary and safe return of internally displaced persons to their places of origin and their smooth re-integration into their societies.

Strongly considering the ratification and full implementation of other ILO conventions concerning the employment rights of minors, women, youth, persons with disabilities, migrants and indigenous peoples. Ensure that migrant workers benefit from the protection provided by relevant national and international instruments, take concrete and effective measures against the exploitation of migrant workers, and encourage all countries to consider the ratification and full implementation of the relevant international instruments on migrant workers, including the International Convention on the Protection of the Rights of All Migrant Workers and Members of Their Families.

References

Baubock, R., Heller, A. & Zolberg,A. (Eds)., "The challenge of diversity: Integration andpluralism in societies of immigration", 1996.

Berry, J.W., "Immigration, acculturation and adaptation", *Applied Psychology*, 1997.

_______________ ., J.S. Phinney, D.L. Sam & P. Vedder (Eds.), "Immigrant youth in culturaltransition: Acculturation, identity and adaptation across national context", Mahwah, NJ:Lawrence Erlbaum Associates, 2006.

United Nations Population Division, *World Immigration Report*, New York, 2002.

8

Population and Health Status

8.1. Introduction

Health and health care need to be distinguished from each other for no better reason than that the former is often incorrectly seen as a direct function of the latter. Heath is clearly not the mere absence of disease. Good Health confers on a person or groups freedom from illness—and the ability to realise one's potential. Health is therefore best understood as the indispensable basis for defining a person's sense of well being. The health of populations is a distinct key issue in public policy discourse in every mature society often determining the deployment of huge society. They include its cultural understanding of ill health and well-being, extent of socio-economic disparities, reach of health services and quality and costs of care and current bio-medical understanding about health and illness.

Health care covers not merely medical care but also all aspects pro preventive care too. Nor can it be limited to care rendered by or financed out of public expenditure-within the government sector alone but must include incentives and disincentives for self care and care paid for by private citizens to get over ill health. Where, as in India, private out-of-pocket expenditure dominates the cost financing health care, the effects are bound to be regressive. Heath care at its essential core is widely recognised to be a public good. Its demand and supply cannot therefore, be left to be regulated solely by the invisible had of the market. Nor can it be established on considerations of utility maximising conduct alone.

8.2. Forecasting in Health Sector

In general predictions about future health—of individuals and populations—can be notoriously uncertain. However all projections of health care in India must in the end rest on the overall changes in its political economy—on progress made in poverty mitigation (health care to the poor) in reduction of inequalities (health inequalities affecting access/quality'), in generation of employment /income streams (to facilitate capacity to pay and to accept individual responsibility for one's health) in public information and development communication and in personal life style changes (often directly resulting from social changes and global influences).

There is a forecast on the new health challenges likely to emerge in India over the next few decades. The key conclusions must be understood keeping in the mind the tact that the concept of DALYs incorporates not only mortality but disability viewed in terms of healthy years of life lost. In this forecast, DALYs are expected to dramatically decrease in respect of diarrhoeal diseases and respiratory infections and less dramatically for maternal conditions. TB is expected to plateau by 2000, and HIV infections are expected to rise significantly up to 2010. Injuries may increase less significantly, the proportion of people above 65 will increase and as a result the burden of no communicable disease will rise. Finally cardiovascular diseases resulting any from the risk associated with smoking urban stress and improper diet are expected to increase dramatically.

Under the same BOD methodology another view is available from a four—state analysis done in 1996 these four states—AP, Kamataka, W. Bengal and Punjab—represent different stages in the Indian health transition. The analysis reveals that the poorer and more populated states. West Bengal, will still face a large incidence of communicable diseases. More prosperous states, such as Punjab further along the health transiting will witness sharply increasing incidence of no communicable diseases especially, in urban areas. The projections highlight that we still operating on unreliable or incomplete base data on mortality and causes of death in the absence of vital registration statistics and know as yet little about how they differ between social classes and regions or about the dynamic patterns of change at work. It also highlights the policy dilemma of how to balance between the articulate middle upper class demand for more access to technologically advanced and subsidised clinical services and the more pressing needs of the poor for coverage of basic disease control interventions. This conflict over deployment of public resources will only get exacerbated in future. What matters most in such estimates are not societal averages with respect to health but sound data illumining specifically the health conditions of the disadvantaged in local areas that long tradition of health sector analysis looking at unequal access, income poverty and unjustly distributed resources as the trigger to meet health needs of the poor. That tradition has been totally replaced by the currently dominant school of international thought about health which is concerned primarily with efficiency of systems measured by cost effectiveness criteria.

8.2.1. Future of State Provided Health Care

Historically the Indian commitment to health development has been guided by two principles-with three consequences. The first principle was State responsibility for health care and the second (after independence) was free medical care for all (and not merely to those unable to pay). The first set of consequences was inadequate priority to public health, poor investment in safe water and sanitation and to the neglect of the key role of personal hygiene in good health, culminating in the persistence of diseases like Cholera.

The second set of consequences pertains to substantially unrealised goals of NHP 1983 due to funding difficulties from compression of public expenditures and from organisational inadequacies. The ambitious and far-reaching NPP—2000 goals and strategies have however been formulated on that edifice in the hope that the gaps and the inadequate would be removed by purposeful action. Without being too defensive or critical about its past failures, the rural health structure should be strengthened and funded and managed efficiently in all States by 2005. This can trigger many dramatically changes over the next twenty years in neglected aspects or rural health and of vulnerable segments.

The third set of consequences appears to be the inability to develop and integrate plural systems of medicine and the failure to assign practical roles to the private sector and to assign public duties for private professionals. To set right these gaps demanded patient redefinition of the state's role keeping the focus on equity.

But during the last decade there has been an abrupt switch to market based governance styles and much influential advocacy to reduce the state role in health in order to enforce overall compression of public expenditure an reduce fiscal deficits. People have therefore been forced to switch between weak and efficient public services and expensive private provision or at the limit forego care entirely except in life threatening situations, in such cases sliding into indebtedness. Health status of any population is not only the record of mortality and its morbidity profile but also a record of its resilience based on mutual solidarity and indigenous traditions of self-care—assets normally invisible to he planner and the professional. Such resilience can be enriched with the State retaining a strategic directional role for the good health of all its citizens in accordance with the constitutional mandate. Within such a framework alone can the private sector be engaged as an additional instrument or a partner for achieving shared public health outcomes. Public programmes in rural and poor urban areas engaging indigenous practitioners and community volunteers can prevent much seasonal and communicable disease using low cost traditional knowledge and based on the balance between food, exercise medicine and moderate living. Such an overall vision of the public role of the heterogeneous private sector must inform the course of future of state led health care in the country.

8.2.2. Key Achievements in Health

A process understanding of longevity and child health may be useful for understanding progress in future. Longevity, always a key national goal, is not merely the reduction of deaths as a result of better medical and rehabilitative care at old age. In fact without reasonable quality of life in the extended years marked by self-confidence and absence of undue dependency longevity may men only a display of technical skills. So quality of life requires as much external bio-medical interventions as culture based acceptance of inevitable decline in faculties without officious start at sixty but run across life lived at all ages in reduction of mortality among infants through immunisation and nutrition interventions and reduction of mortality among young and middle aged adults, including adolescents getting inform about sexuality reproduction and safe motherhood. At the same time, some segments will remain always more vulnerable—such as women due to patriarchy and traditions of infra-family denial), aged (whose survival but not always development will increase with immunisation) and the disabled (constituting a tenth of the population).

Reduction in child mortality involves as much attention to protecting children from infection as in ensuring nutrition and calls for a holistic view of mother and child health services. The cluster of services consisting of antenatal services, delivery care and post mortem attention and low birth weight, childhood diarrhoea and ARI management are linked priorities. Programme of immunisation and childhood nutrition seen in better performing status indicate sustained attention to routine and complex investments into growing children as a group to make them grow into persons capable of living long and well Often interest fades in pursuing the unglamorous routine of supervised immunisation and is substituted by pulse campaigns etc. Which in the long run turn out counter-productive. Indeed persistence with improved routines and care for quality in immunisation would also be a pathway to reduce the world's highest rate of maternal mortality.

The initial key mistake arose from the needless bifurcation of health and family welfare and nutrition functions at all levels instead of promoting more holism. As a result of all this the structure has been precluded from reaching its optimal potential. It has got more firmly established at the periphery/subcenter level and dedicated to RCH services only. At PHC and CHC levels this has further been compounded by a weak referral system. There has not been enough convergence in "escorting" children through immunisation coverage and nutrition education of mothers and ensuring better food to children, including cooked midday meals and health checks at schools. There has also been no constructive engagement between allopathic and indigenous systems to build synergies, which could have improved people's perceptions of benefits from the infrastructure in ways that made sense to them.

One key task in the coming decades is therefore to utilise fully that created potential by attending to well known organisational motivational and financial gaps. The gaps have arisen partly from the source and scale of funds and partly due to lack of persistence, both of which can be set right. PHCs and CHCs are funded by States several of whom are unable to match Central assistance offered and hence these centers remain inadequate and operate on minimum efficiency. On the other hand over two thirds cost of three fourths of sub-centers are fully met by the Centre due to their key role m family welfare services. But in equal part these gaps are due to many other non-monetary factors such as undue centralisation and uniformity, fluctuating commitment to key routines at ground level, insufficient experimentation with alternatives such as getting public duties discharged through private professionals and ensuring greater local accountability to users.

8.3. Health Status Issues

The difference between rural and urban indicators of health status and the wide interstate disparity in health status are well known. Clearly the urban rural differentials are substantial and range from childhood and go on increasing the gap as one grows up to 5 years. In spite of overall achievement it is a mixed record of social development specially failing in involving people in imaginative ways. Even the averaged out good performance ides wide variations by social class or gender or region or State. The classes in may States have had to suffer the most due to lack of access or denial of access or social exclusion or all of them.

8.3.1. Combating Disease

The remarkable success in China in combating disease is due to sustained attention on the health of the young in China, and of public policy backed by resources and social mobilisation- While comparing China and India in selected aspects of disease load, demography and public expenditures on health, the record on India may seem mixed compared to the more all round progress made by china. But this should also be seen in the perspective of the larger burden of disease in India compared to china and of the transactional costs of an open and free democracy.

8.3.2. Major Disease Control Efforts

A careful analysis of the Global Burden of Disease (GBD) study focusing on age specific morbidity during 2000 in ten most common diseases (excluding injuries) shows that sixty percent of morbidity is due to infectious diseases and common tropical diseases, a quarter due to life-style disorders and 13% due to potentially preventable prenatal conditions. Apart from the above, there remains a vast unfinished burden in preventing controlling or eliminating other major communicable diseases and in bringing down the risk of deaths in maternal and peri-natal conditions. Endemic diseases arising from infection or lack of nutrition continue to account for almost two thirds of morality and morbidity India.

8.3.2.1. Tuberculosis

TB is a wide spread disease of poverty among women living and working in ill ventilated places and other undernourished persons in urban slums it is increasingly affecting the younger adults also in the economically productive segments. No universal screening is possible. Sputum positive test does not precede diagnosis but drugs are prescribed on the basis of fever and shadows as a result incomplete cure becomes common and delayed tests only prove the wrong diagnosis too late. Improved diagnosis through better training and clear protocols and elimination of drug resistance through incomplete cure should be priority. The DOTS programme trying for full compliance after proper diagnosis is settling down but already has some claims of success. More tan 3000 laboratories have been set up for diagnosis and about 1.5 lakh workers trained and with total population coverage by 2007 cure rates (already claimed to have doubled) may rise substantially. There is reason to hope that DOTS programmes would prove a greater success over time with increased community awareness generation.

The key issue is how soon and how well can it be integrated into the PHC system and made subject to routines of local accountability, without which no low cost regime of total compliance is feasible in a country as large as India. An optimistic assessment could be that with commitment and full use of infrastructure it will be possible to arrest further growth in absolute numbers of TB cases keeping it at below 1.5 million till 2010 even though the population will be growing. Once that is done TB can be brought down to less than a million lie within internationally accepted limits and disappears as a major communicable disease in India by 2020.

8.3.2.2. Malaria

As regards malaria, we have had a long record of success and failure and each intervention has been thwarted by new problems and plagued by recrudescence. At present India has a large manpower fully aware of all aspects of malaria about often low in motivation. It can be transformed into a large-scale work force for awareness generation, tests and distribution of medicine.

There is growing interest and community awareness of biological methods of control of mosquito growth. Unfortunately diligent ground level public health work is in grave disarray in these areas but can be improved by better supervision greater use of panchayatraj institutions and buildings on modest demonstrated successes. As regards a vaccine, there seems to be no sufficient incentive for international R&D to focus on a relatively lower priority or research. Roll back malaria programmes of the WHO are more likely to concentrate on Africa whose profile of malaria is not similar to ours. The search for a vaccine continues but has little likelihood of immediate success. In spite of various difficulties, if the restructuring of the malaria work force and the strengthening of health infrastructure takes place, one can expect that the incidence can be reduced by a third or even upto half in the next decade or so. For this it is necessary that routine tasks like timely spraying and logistics for taking blood slides testing and their analysis and organic methods of reducing mosquito spread etc.

8.3.2.3. AIDS

There would hopefully be wider consultation with persons with caring sensibilities including AIDS patients on how to counsel in different eventualities and to get the balance right between hospital and home care and how to develop a humane affordable policy for anti retroviral drugs for AIDS patients. The matter involves a true dilemma, for public health priorities themselves certainly argue for more funds should address diseases constituting bigger population based hazards. Investments made m such expensive interventions can instead be made in supporting hospice efforts in the voluntary and private sectors.

Whatever position may emerge in research or spread of infection of case fatalities, a multi pronged attempt for awareness, must continue and tough choices must get discussed openly without articulate special, often urban middle class interests denying other views and especially public health priorities of the poor. The promotion of barrier protection must increase but has to related to a system of values, which would be acceptable to the people's beliefs. We need to strengthen sentinel surveillance systems and awareness effort. In any case many of the ill cannot afford the high prices or have access to it from public agencies. The strict patent regimen under TRIPS is bound to prevail, notwithstanding the ambivalently worded Doha decision of WTO that public health emergencies provide sufficient cause of countries to use the flexibility available from various provisions of TRIPS.

8.3.3. Maternal and Parental Deaths

Maternal and parental deaths are sizeable but the advantage here is that they can be prevented merely by more intensive utilisation of existing rural health infrastructure. Policy and implementation must keep steady focus on key items such as improved institutional deliveries better-trained birth attendants and timely antenatal screening to eliminate anaemia and at the same time isolate cases needing referral or other targeted attention. After all Tamil Nadu has by such methods ensured closed to 90% institutional deliveries backed by a functional referral. Firm administrative will and concurrent supervision of specified screening tasks included in MCH services can give us a window of opportunity to dramatically bring down within a few years alarming maternal mortality currently one of the highest in the world.

There can be a systematic campaign over five years to increase institutional deliveries as near as possible to the Tamil Nadu level, also taking into account assisted, home deliveries by trained staff with doctors at call. For the interim TBAs should be relied on through a mass awareness campaign involving Gram Panchayats too. Over a period of time there is no reason why ANMs entitled benefits of children to help in their growth and not remain as welfare measure. Using the infrastructures fully and with community participation and extensive social mobilisation many tasks in nutrition are feasible and can be in position to make impact by 2010.

8.3.4. Child Health and Nutrition

Associated with this is the issue of infant and child mortality, and low birth weight most mortality occurs from diarrhoea and the stagnation in IMR in the last few year is bound to have a negative effect on population stabilisation goals. As regards childhood diarrhoea, deaths are totally preventable simple community action and public education by targeting children of low birth weights and detecting early those children at risk from malnutrition through proper low cost screening procedure, the present arrangement has got too burdened with attempting total population coverage getting all children weighed even once in three months and making ANMs depots for ORS and for simple drugs for fever and motivating the community to take pride in healthy children are the lessons of the success of the Tamil Nadu Nutrition Project. The success can be built upon till 2025 for reaching levels comparable to China. Concentration on preventive measures of maternal and child health and in particular improved nutrition services will be particularly useful because it will help that generation to have a head start in good health who are going to be a part of the demographic bonus.

To ensure best results in this stage the present nutritional services must be converted into targeted (and entitled) benefits of children to help in their growth and not remain as welfare measure. Using the infrastructures fully and with community participation and extensive social mobilisation many tasks in nutrition are feasible and can be in position to make impact by 2010. Mild and moderate malnutrition still prevalent in over half of our young population can be halved if food as the supplemental pathway to better nutrition becomes a priority both for self reliance and lower costs. There has been a tendency for micro nutrient supplementation to overwhelm food derived nourishment. This trend is assisted by foreign aid but over a long run may prove unsustainable- By engaging the adolescents into proper nutrition education and reproductive health awareness we can seamlessly weave into the nutritional security system of our country a corps of informed interconnected and imaginative ideas can be tried out.

8.4. Health Infrastructure

Issues in regard to public and private health infrastructure are different and both of them need attention but in different ways. Rural public infrastructure must remain in mainstay for wider access to health care for all without imposing undue burden on them. Side by side the existing set of public hospitals at district and sub-district levels must be supported by good management and with adequate funding and user fees and out contracting services, all as part of a functioning referral net work. This demands better routines more accountable staff and attention to promote quality. Many reputed public hospitals have suffered from lack of autonomy inadequate budgets for non-wage O&M leading to faltering and poorly motivated care. All these are being tackled in several states are part health sector reform, and will reduce the waste involved in simpler cases needlessly reaching tertiary hospitals direct These, attempts must persist without any wavering or policy changes or periodic denigration of their past working. More autonomy to large hospitals and district public health authorities will enable them to plan and implement decentralised and flexible and locally controlled services and remove the dichotomy between hospital and primary care services.

The PHC approach as implemented seems to have strayed away from its key thrust in preventive and public health action. No system exists for purposeful community focused public information or seasonal alerts or advisories or community health information to be circulated among doctors in both private practice and in public sector. PHCs were meant to be local epidemiological information centers, which could develop simple community.

Tertiary hospitals had been given concessional land, customs exemption and liberal tax breaks against a commitment to reserve beds for poor patients for free treatments. No procedures exist to monitor this and the disclosure systems are far from transparent, redressal of patient grievances is poor and allegations of cuts and commissions to promote needless procedure are common.

The bulk of noncorporate private entities such as nursing homes are run by doctors and doctors- entrepreneurs and remain unregulated either in terms of facility of competence standards or quality and accountability of practice and sometimes operate without systematic medical records and audits. Medical education has become more expensive and with rapid technological advances in medicine, specialisation has more attractive rewards. Indeed the reward expectations of private practice formerly spread out over career long earnings are squeezed into a few years, which becomes possible only by working in hi-tech hospital some times run as businesses. The responsibilities or private sector in clinical and preventive public health services were not specified though under the NHP 1983 nor during the last decade of reforms followed up either by government of profession by any strategy to engage allocate, monitor and regulate such private provision nor assess the costs and benefits or subsidisation of private hospitals. There has been talk of public private partnerships, but this has yet to take concrete shape by imposing pubic duties on private professionals, wherever there is agreement on explicitly public health outcomes. In fact it has required the Supreme Court to lay down the professional obligations of private doctors in accidents and injuries who used to be refused treatment in case of potential becoming part of a criminal offence.

The respective roles of the public and private sectors in health care has been a key issue in debate over a long time. As regards the poor with priced services. Taking into account the size of the burden, the clinical and public health services cannot be shouldered for all by government alone. The distribution of the burden, between the two sectors would depend on the shape and size of the social pyramid in each society. There is no objection to introduce user fees, contractual arrangements, risk pooling, etc for mobilisation of resources for health care. But, the line should be drawn not so much between public and private roles, but between institutions and health care run as businesses or run in a wider public interest as a social enterprise with economic dimensions. In a market economy, health care is subject to three links, none of which should become out of balance with the other—the link between state and citizens' entitlement for health, the link between the consumer and provider of health services and the link between the physician and patient.

8.4.1. Medicinal Practice in Private Sector

Over the last several decades, independent private medical practice has become widespread but has remained stubbornly urban with polyclinics, nursing homes and hospitals proliferating often through doctor entrepreneurs. At our level tertiary hospitals in major cities are in may cases run by business houses and use corporate business strategies and hi-tech specialisation to create demand and attract those with effective demand or the critically vulnerable at increasing costs. Standards in some of them are truly world class and some who work there are outstanding leaders in their areas. But given the commodification of medical care as part of a business plan it has not been possible to regulate the quality, accountability and fairness in care through criteria for accreditation, transparency in fees, medical audit, accountable record keeping, credible grievance procedures etc. such accreditation, standard setting and licensure systems are best done under self regulation, but self regulation systems in India medical practice have been deficient in many respects creating problem in credibility. Acute care has become the key priority and continues to attract manpower and investment into related speciality education and facilities for technological improvement. Common treatments, inexpensive diagnostic procedures and family medicine are replaced and priced out of the reach of most citizens in urban areas.

8.4.1.1. Private expenditure trends

When services are provided by private sector it is largely for ambulatory care and less for inpatient carte. There are variations in levels of cost, pricing, transactional conveniences and quality of services. There is evidence to suggest that disparities in income as such do not make a difference in meeting health care costs, except for catastrophic or life threatening situations.

Privatisation has to be distinguished from private medical practice, which has always been substantial within our mixed economy. There are complex reasons for this trend. First is the high scarcity cost of good medical education, and second the reward differential between public and corporate tertiary hospitals leading to the reluctance of the young professional to be lured away from the market to public service in rural areas and finally there is the compulsion of returns on investment whenever expensive equipment in installed as part of practice. Increasingly, this has shifted the balance from individual practice to institutionalises practice, in hospitals, polyclinics. This in turn induces increases in insurance premiums making such cover beyond the capacity to pay. There is a distinct possibility of such cycles of cost escalation periodically occurring in the future, promoted further by global transfer of knowledge and software, tele-medicine etc. especially after the advent of predictive medicine and gene manipulation.

Doctors practicing in the private sector are sometimes accused of prescribing excessive, expensive medicines and with using rampant and less than justified use of technology for diagnosis and treatment. Some method of accreditation of hospitals and facilities and better licensure systems of doctors is likely within a decade. This will enables some moderation in levels of charges in using new technology. High cost of care is sometimes sought to be justified as necessary due to defensive medicine practiced in order to meet risks under the Consumer Protection Act.

As health insurance gets established it may impost more stringent criteria and restrictions on physician performance, which may tempt them into defensive medicine. There may also be attempt to collusive capture and (indirect ownership) of insurance companies by corporate hospitals as in other countries. Advances in medical technology are rapid and dominant and easily travel world wide and often seen as good investment and brand equity in the private sector. Private independent practices—and to smaller extent hospitals, dispensaries, nursing homes tele-are seen as markets for medical services with each segment seeking to maximise gains and build mutually supporting links with other segments.

Appropriate regulation is likely in the next decade for minimum standards and accountability and that should consist of a balanced mix of self-regulation external regulation by standard setting and accreditation agencies including private voluntary health insurance. It includes risk pooling initiatives for sharing costs among the healthy and the sick leading to insurance schemes as a substitute for or as supplementary to State provision for minimum uniform services. It also covers risk-sharing initiatives across wealth and income involving public policy decisions on progressive taxation, merit subsidy and cross subsidisation by dual pricing. Both will continue to be necessary in our conditions with more emphasis on risk sharing as growth picks up. Risk pooling within private voluntary and mandated insurance schemes has become inevitable in all countries because of the double burden of sickness and to ensure that financial costs of treatment do not become an excessive burden relative to incomes. It is difficult but necessary to embed these notions of fair financing into legislation, regulations and schemes and programs equity is aimed at in health care.

Insurance is a welcome necessary step and must doubtless expand to help in facilitating equitable health care to shift to sections for which government is responsible. Indeed for those not able to access insurance it is government that will have to continue to provide the minimum services, and intervene against market failures including denial through adverse selection or moral hazard. Indeed in the long run the degree of inequity in health care after insurance systems are set up will depend ironically on the strength and delivery of the public system as a counterpoise in holding costs and relevance in technology.

The insurance regulatory authority has announced priority in licensing to companies set up with health insurance as key business and has emphasised the need for developing new products on fair terms to those at risk among the poor and in rural areas. Much will turn on what progress takes place through sound regulation covering aspects indicated below. In order to be socially relevant and commercially viable the scheme must aim at a proper mix of health hazards and cover many broad social classes and income groups. Innovative community based new products can be developed by using the scattered experience of such products for instance in SEWA, so that a minimum core cover can be developed as a model for innovative insurance by panchayats with re-insurance backup by companies and government bearing part of promotional costs.

The bulk of the formal sector maybe covered by an expanded mandatory insurance with affordable cover and convenient modes of premium payment. Outside the formal manufacturing sector innovate schemes can be designed around specific occupation groups in the informal sector which are steadily becoming a base for old age pension entitlements, as in Kerala and Tamil Nadu—and brought under common risk rating. Finally, as in the West health insurance should develop influence and capacity as bulk purchaser or medical and hospital services to impact on quality and cost and provide greater understanding about Indian health and illness behaviours, patterns of utilisation of care and intra family priorities for accessing medical care. Health insurance should be welcomed as a force for a fairer healthcare system. But its success should be judged on how well new products are developed with a cover beyond hospitalisation, how fairly and inclusively the cover is offered and how far community rated premiums are established.

8.5. Health Perceptions and Plural Systems

Health perceptions play an important part in ensuring sound health outcomes. To a large extent they are culturally determined but also subject to change with economic growth and social development. People intuitively develop capacity to make choices are being treated under the western of indigenous systems of medicines, keep a balance between good habits traditionally developed for healthy living and modem lifestyles, decide on where to go for chrome and acute care and how to apportion intra-family utilisation of healthcare resources.

Improvement in the health status of the population has been one of the major thrust areas for the social development programmes of the country. This was to be achieved through improving the access to and utilisation of Health services with special focus on under served and under privileged segments of the population. Over the last five decades, India has built up a vast health infrastructure and manpower at primary, secondary and tertiary care in government, voluntary and private sectors. Professionals and para-professionals trained in the medical colleges in modern medicine and ISM&H and para-professional training institutions man these institutions. The population has become aware of the benefits of health related technologies for prevention, early diagnosis and effective treatment for a wide variety of illnesses and accessed available services. Technological advances and improvement in access to health care technologies, which were relatively inexpensive and easy to implement, had resulted in substantial improvement in health indices of the population and a steep decline in mortality. The extent of access to and utilisation of health care varied substantially between states, districts and different segments of society; this to a large extent, is responsible for substantial differences between states in health indices of the population.

During the 1990s, the mortality rates reached a plateau and the country entered an era of dual disease burden. Communicable diseases have become more difficult to combat because of development of insecticide resistant strains of vectors, antibiotics resistant strains of bacteria and emergence of HIV infection for which there is no therapy. Longevity and changing life style have resulted in the increasing prevalence of non-communicable diseases. Under nutrition, micro nutrient deficiencies and associated health problems coexist with obesity and non-communicable diseases. The existing health system suffers from inequitable distribution of institutions and manpower. Even though the country produces over 17,000 doctors in modern system of medicine and similar number of ISM&H practitioners and para-professionals, there are huge gaps in critical manpower in institutions providing primary healthcare, especially in the remote rural and tribal areas where health care needs are the greatest.

As the country undergoes demographic and epidemiological transition, it is likely that larger investments in health will be needed even to maintain the current health status because tackling resistant infections and non-communicable diseases will inevitably lead to escalating health care costs. Last two decades have witnessed explosive expansion in expensive health care related technologies, broadening diagnostic and therapeutic avenues. Increasing awareness and rising expectations to access these have widened the gap between what is possible and what is affordable for the individual or the country. Policy makers and programme managers realise that in order to address the increasingly complex situation regarding access to good quality care at affordable costs, it is essential to build up an integrated health system with appropriate screening, regulating access at different levels and efficient referral linkages. However, both health care providers and health care seekers still feel more comfortable with the one to one relationship with each other than with the health system approach.

Another problem is the popular perception that curative and preventive care competes for available resources, with the former getting preference in funding. Efforts to convince the public that preventive and curative care are both part of the entire spectrum of health care ranging from health promotion, specific protection, early diagnosis and prompt treatment, disability limitation and rehabilitation and that to improve the health status of the population both are equally essential have not been very successful. Traditionally health service (both government and private) was perceived as a social responsibility albeit a paid one. Growing commercialisation of health care and medical education over the last two decades has eroded this commitment, adversely affecting the quality of care, trust and the rapport between health care seekers and providers.

8.5.1. Human Resource Development for Health

During new century medical education faces newer opportunities and challenges. The country has to train an adequate number of health professionals with appropriate knowledge, skill and attitude to meet the health care needs of the growing population and dual disease burden.

In this era of globalisation, India with its excellent teachers and abundant clinical material can become a key player in medical education. The health care institutions can transform India into a major medical tourism destination. Appropriate investment in research and development and quality control can result in a massive expansion of the pharmaceutical sector. The next two decades will show whether the country has successfully used these opportunities to train and provide gainful employment to the highly skilled medical manpower improving community awareness, participation and effective utilisation of available services; use of PRIs in improving community participation and monitoring implementation of programmes.

8.5.2. Indian Systems of Medicine and Homoeopathy

The Indian Systems of Medicine and Homoeopathy consist of Ayurveda, Siddha, Unani and Homoeopathy, and therapies such as Yoga and Naturopathy. Some of these systems are indigenous and others such as Homeopathy have over the years become a part of Indian tradition. Prior to the advent of modern medicine these systems had, for centuries, catered to the health care needs of the people; these systems are widely used even today because their practitioners are acceptable both geographically and culturally, are accessible and their services and drugs are affordable.

8.5.3. Communicable and Non-Communicable Diseases

Appropriate strategies for combating the dual disease burden for prevention, detection and management of communicable and non-communicable disease through existing health care infrastructure will be evolved, implemented and evaluated. Modalities to improve delivery of services pertaining to these programmes through the existing health services should be worked out. Efforts will be made to improve states ownership of the programmes, participation of the community, private sector and NGOs. Local accountability and intersectoral co-ordination should be improved through the involvement of PRIs. Evaluation and operational research to rectify problems in implementation and improving efficiency will receive attention.

Appropriate modification will be required in the health care delivery as the country undergoes demographic and epidemiological transition and non-communicable disease emerges as major public health problems. In view of this there is a need to obtain data on not only mortality but also morbidity due to chronic illnesses and disabilities and take them into account while formulating public health programmes. There are wide inter-state differences health indices, morbidity rates and rate of demographic and epidemiological transition.

8.5.4. Medical Research

Medical research can play a major role in improving access to health care. In India, most of the morbidity and mortality is due to illnesses for which simple, inexpensive and effective preventive measures and time-tested cost-effective curative interventions are available. Therefore, priority has been given to health systems research for improving service delivery and coverage as well as operational research aimed at improving access to technological advances. Basic and clinical research leading to development of products, drugs, vaccines for prevention, diagnosis and management of illnesses especially major health problems for which currently there is no effective cure are encouraged. Health policy research and health system research at the national level is essential and a reliable information base is a pre-condition for effective investment in health care and performance assessment of the health system.

Currently, Indian industry is investing about 5 per cent of turnover on research and development. These investments may have to be augmented so that the Indian pharmaceutical industry achieves its full potential. Parallel efforts to improve public sector-funded research are also essential for the development of drugs for the treatment of public health problems such as emerging drug resistance, development of newer contraceptives and vaccines. The private sector may not be willing to make requisite investments in these areas because of very low profit margins.

8.6. Financing Health Care

As a part of economic reforms health sector reforms are perhaps inevitable; however due care will be taken to ensure that poorer segments of population are able to access services they need. In view of the importance of health as a critical input for human development there will be continued commitment to provide essential primary health care, emergency life saving services, services under the National disease control programmes and the National Family Welfare programme totally free of cost to individuals based on their needs and not on their ability to pay.

The issue of how much the government sector, private individuals and the country as a whole is spending on health care and which segments of the population are benefiting has been debated widely during the last decade. As there is no National Health Accounting system, there is no information on total government expenditure on health and categories of people who benefit from this expenditure. It is imperative that a system of National Health Accounting, reflecting total government expenditure on health is established. This will enable periodic review and appropriate policy decisions regarding modalities for ensuring optimal utilisation of the current government investment in the health sector and also future investments to meet public health needs.

8.6.1. Family Welfare

India, the second most populous country in the world having a meagre 2.4% of the world's surface area sustains 16.7% of the world's population. Realising the inevitable high population growth during the initial phases of demographic transition and the need to accelerate the pace of the transition, India became the first country in the world to formulate a National Family Planning Programme in 1952, with the objective of "reducing birth rate to the extent necessary to stabilise the population at a level consistent with requirement of national economy". The First Five Year Plan stated "The main appeal for family planning is based on considerations of health and welfare of the family. Family limitation or spacing of children is necessary and desirable in order to secure better health for the mother and better care and upbringing of children. Measures directed to this end should, therefore, form part of the public health programme". Thus the key elements of health care to women and children and provision of contraceptive services have been the focus of India's health services right from the time of India's independence. Successive Five Year Plans have been providing the policy framework and funding for planned development of nationwide health care infrastructure and manpower to deliver these services. The centrally sponsored and 100% centrally funded Family Welfare Programme provides the States additional infrastructure, manpower and consumables needed for improving health status of women and children and to meet all the felt needs for fertility regulation.

In order to give a new thrust and dynamism to the Family Welfare Programme and achieve a more rapid decline in birthrate, death rate and population growth rate in the last decade of the century, the National Development Council (NDC) set up a Sub-Committee on Population and endorsed its recommendations in 1993.

8.6.2. Nutrition

Importance of optimal nutrition for health and human development is well recognised. At the time of Independence the country faced two major nutritional problems—one was the threat of famine and acute starvation due to low agricultural production and lack of appropriate food distribution system.

The country adopted multi-sectoral, multi-pronged strategy to combat these and to improve nutritional status of the population. Constitution of India (Article 47) states that "the State shall regard raising the level of nutrition and standard of living of its people and improvement in public health among its primary duties". Successive Five-Year Plans laid down the policies and strategies for achieving these goals. During the last 50 years considerable progress has been achieved.

8.7. Conclusion

During the next two decades the will have to implement focused and comprehensive interventions aimed at improving the nutritional status of the individuals; this in turn will enable the country to achieve rapid reduction in severer forms of under-nutrition and ill health and lead to improvement in nutritional and health status of the population to achieve this objective, coordinated multi sectoral interventions for increasing food production, effective processing and distribution, improvement in purchasing power, generating awareness, ensuring optimum utilisation of well targeted interventions for prevention, detection and management of macro and micronutrient deficiencies are needed.

References

Bold, "Health Status of Elderly in India" *International Institute of Ageing*, United Nations, Malta, 2001

Gupta, I., P. Dasgupta and M. Sawhney, " Health of the Elderly in India: Some Aspects of Vulnerability" *Discussion paper series No 26*, Institute of Economic Growth, University Enclave, Delhi-7, 2001.

Reddy, P. H., " The health of the aged in India", *Health Transition Review*, 1996.

9

Population Poverty and Environment

9.1. Introduction

There is widespread impression among the Indian intelligentsia, foreign scholars and residents of developed/rich countries that India's economic growth has not reduced poverty, that globalisation has worsened poverty and/or income distribution and there are 100 of millions of hungry people in India. These arguments are buttressed by recourse to India's ranking on several social indicators.

The growth of population in certain areas, through both net migration and national increase, had accelerated the rates that could frustrate all the efforts to conquer poverty and underdevelopment and to maintain a safe and stable environment.

Rapid population growth and poverty in country is adversely affecting the environment. As the 21st century begins, growing number of people and rising levels of consumption per capita are depleting natural resources and degrading the environment. In India, the rapid increase of population combines with desperate poverty to deplete and pollute local resource bases on which the livelihood of present and future generations depends. Though the relationship is complex, population size and growth tend to expand and accelerate these human impacts on the environment. What is more concern, the number of population rise will increase to such an extent in future that it will cause overall scarcity for resources.

India is having 18 per cent of the world's population on 2.4 per cent of its land area has great deal of pressure on its all natural resources. It is now well accepted that population, poverty, the economy and environment are interconnected. Poverty and general lack of access to capital, resources and technology contribute to deforestation. The population pressures can leads to resource degradation and poverty. There is a growing emphasis that economic policies also affect poverty and environment, be it direct or indirect, bearing on the availability as well as utilisation of natural resources.

The growing population has forced poor villagers to deforest and cultivate the deforested land for agricultural purposes and to meet their livelihood needs. The poor are both agents and victims of deforestation. Undoubtedly, clearing of forests for agricultural purposes will increase income but this is not without any other side effects. The continuing need for family labour supports high fertility and rapid population growth. Continued deforestation will have grave consequences for the health of both humans and ecosystems. The consequences of unrelenting population growth on natural resources depletion and environmental degradation are not easily dealt with.

The lack of knowledge is a problem. Thus, there is a need to promote public awareness of the linkages between population, poverty and environment. Environmentalists and economists increasingly agree that efforts to protect the environment and to achieve better living standards can be closely linked and are mutually reinforcing. Slowing the increase in population, especially in the face of rising per capita demand for natural resources, can take pressure off the environment and buy time to improve living standards on a sustainable basis. Though the relationship is complex, population size and growth tend to expand and accelerate these human impacts on the natural resources and environment. All these in turn lead to an increase in the pollution levels.

However, environmental pollution not only leads to deteriorating environmental conditions but also have adverse effects on the sustainable development and health of people. What is more concern, the number of population rise will increase to such an extent in future that it will cause overall scarcity for resources. India is having 16.87 per cent of the world's population on 2.4 per cent of its land area has great deal of pressure on its all natural resources including land. The increase of population has been tending towards alarming situation. The world's population was estimated to be 6.056 billion in mid 2000 and projected 7.936 billion in the year 2025 and 9.322 was estimated to be 6.056 billion in mid 2000 and projected 7.936 billion in the year 2025 and 9.322 billion in the·year 2050. The projected population indicates that India will be most populous country in the world and China will be second in 2050. If the population continues to multiply, the impact on environment could be devastating. What is more concern, the rise in population will increase to such an extent in future that it will cause overall scarcity for resources. The deficiency of natural resources will furthermore create environmental hazards in the world. Decades of economic expansion and population growth have degraded its land, air and water.

9.2. Population Growth in India

India is the second most populous country in the world after China. The population of India has crossed the one billion marks. According to the provisional results of the Census of India 2001, the population of India on 1st March 2001 is 1029 millions. At the time of independence, the country's population was 342 million. The number has multiplied three-fold in around five decades.

The total population size of India had grown from 361 million in 1951 to around 1027 million in 2001. The population of India increased by more than 2.8 times during the period of 1951-2001. It is estimated that the country's population will increase to 1.26 billion by the year 2016. The rural population of India has increased around two and half times from 298.7 to 741.7 million during 1951-2001, whereas the urban population has grown 4.6 fold from 62.4 million in 1951 to 285.3 million in 2001. The decadal growth rates of the population are irregular, as it increased from 13.31 per cent in 1951 to 24.8 per cent in 1971. It marginally declined to 24.7 per cent in 1981, 23.8 per cent in 1991 and 21.35 per cent in 2001. The rural decadal growth rate of population varies from 8.79 per cent in 1951 to 20.01 per cent in 1991 and 17.97 per cent in 2001, whereas the urban decadal growth rate of population varies from 41.43 per cent in 1951 to 36.47 per cent in 1991 and 31.11 per cent in 2001. There are various reasons for this variation in the trend of population growth rate in various censuses. The increase in population has been due to the improvement in health conditions and control of diseases. The density of population has gone up from 117 in 1951 to 267 persons in 1991 to 312 persons in 2001 and it always shows an increasing trend over the census years in persons per square kilometer.

Several push and pull factors are presumed to be operative towards distress out migration from rural to urban areas. This might be due to the declining resource availability per capita and shrinking economic opportunities in rural areas, and better economic opportunities, health and educational facilities etc. in urban areas, providing opportunities for higher level of human capital development could be the underlying factors for rural out migration.

9.2.1. Vital Rates in India

The growth of population depends upon fertility, mortality and migration. The process of accelerated population growth in India till 1970s were observed to witness a marginal deceleration during 1980s, as the decadal population growth was 23.9 per cent compared to 24.9 per cent in 1970s. Further declines in fertility have been witnessed during 1990s.

Birth rate in India has declined from 33.9 per thousand populations in 1981 to 29 per thousand populations in 1991 and it further declined to 25 per thousand populations in 2001. At the same time crude death rate has also declined from 12.5 per thousand populations in 1981 to 9.8 per thousand populations in 1991 and it further declined to 8 per thousand populations in 2001. Thus, the natural growth rate of India's population has declined from 21.4 per cent in 1981 to 17 per cent in 2001. The Total fertility rate has also declined from 4.5 children per women in 1981 to 3.1 children per women in 2001. Infant Mortality Rate (IMR) per thousand in India has steadily declined from 110 in 1981 to 72 in 1991 but the present IMR (66) is still very high.

9.3. Poverty and its Environmental Effects

Most of India's poor live in rural areas and are engaged in agriculture. India's poverty reduction through the anti-poverty and employment generation programmes along with overall economic growth planning efforts has helped to reduce the

Poverty is said to be both cause and effect of environment degradation. The poor people, who rely on natural resources more than the rich, deplete natural resources faster as they have no real prospects of gaining access to other types of resources. Poorer people, who cannot meet their subsistence needs through purchase, are forced to use common property resources such as forests for food and fuel, pastures for fodder, and ponds and rivers for water. Population pressure driven overexploitation of the surface and underground water resources by the poor has resulted into contamination and exhaustion of the water resources. Urban population is also using rivers to dispose of untreated sewage and industrial effluent. The result is that health of those dependents on untreated water resources is increasing at risk. In the absence of capital resources, the poor are directly dependent on natural resources. Moreover degraded environment can accelerate the process of impoverishment, again because the poor depend directly on natural assets.

Acceleration in poverty alleviation is imperative to break this link between poverty and the environment. The poverty and rapid population growth are found to coexist and thus seems to reinforcing each other. It also contributes to environmental degradation through over exploitation of natural resources like land, air and water. The deterioration of natural resources and unsafe living conditions affects the environment and health of the poor people.

The creation of employment opportunities is essential in agricultural areas with high poverty, unemployment and landlessness. Poverty, by reducing incentives for long-term resource management, can deplete the natural resources. Environment degradation, in turn, lessens the labour productivity of poor and the productivity of natural resources they manage. Poor people to meet their needs over-exploit the natural resources. Poverty also affects the demographic characteristics of the population and hinders the transition to slower population growth.

9.3.1. Land Utilisation Patterns in India

A change in land utilisation pattern implies an increase or decrease in the proportion of area under different land uses at a point in two or more time periods. The extent of agricultural intensification and extensification characterized by increase in cropping and irrigation intensity and higher use of chemical fertilisers, pesticides and insecticides. The process of agricultural extensification and intensification is leading to land degradation, overexploitation of underground water resources, increased use of chemical fertilisers leading to eutrophication and water pollution. Agricultural intensification because of increasing cropping intensity, irrigation intensity and excessive use of chemical fertilisers resulting into water logging, salinisation and alkalinisation of croplands and eutrophication of water bodies and ill health of oceans and thus reductions in biodiversity.

9.3.2. Forest Resources

Forests are an important natural resource of India. They play an important role in providing raw materials to industries and generating income and employment. Forests also play an important role in enhancing the quality of environment by influencing the ecological balance and life support system (checking soil erosion, maintaining soil fertility, conserving water, regulating water cycles and floods, balancing carbon dioxide and oxygen content in atmosphere etc. They have moderate influence against floods and thus they protect the soil erosion. Per capita availability of forests in India is much lower than the world average. In the year 2001, as compared to 1999, the total forest cover had increased by 38.24 thousand Sq. Kms. The states which shown significant increase in forest covers which shown significant increase in forest covers are Bihar, Himachal Pradesh, Karnataka, Tamil Nadu, Gujarat, Maharashtra, Punjab, West Bengal and Rajasthan. However, it has increased in 1999 by 3.90 thousand Sq. Kms. as compared to 1997. In the year 1997, as compared to 1993, the total forest cover has decreased by 6.71 thousand Sq. Kms. The states, which have shown significant decline in the forest covers, are Andhra Pradesh and Madhya Pradesh. Whereas the states of Gujrat, Maharashtra, Rajasthan and West Bengal have shown an increase in forest cover.

9.3.3. Land/Soil Degradation

Direct impacts of agricultural development on the environment arise from farming activities, which contribute to soil erosion, land salination and loss of nutrients. The spread of green revolution has been accompanied by over exploitation of land and water resources and use of fertilisers and pesticides have increased many folds. Shifting cultivation has also been an important cause of land degradation. Leaching from extensive use of pesticides and fertilisers is an important source of contamination of water bodies. Intensive agriculture and irrigation contribute to land degradation particularly salination, alkalisation and water logging. It is evident that most of the land in the country is degrading, thus affecting the productive resource base of the economy.

9.3.4. Soil Erosion and Land Degradation

Water and wind erosion is the major contributor of 141.3 million hectares to soil erosion, with other factors like water logging 8.5 million hectares, alkali soil 3.6 million hectares, acid soil 4.5 million hectares, saline soil including coastal sandy areas 5.5 million hectares adding to the situ degradation. While soil erosion by rain and river in hill areas causes landslides and floods, deforestation, overgrasing, traditional agricultural practices, mining and incorrect siting of development projects in forest areas have resulted in opening up of these areas to heavy soil erosion. Ravines and gullies reported 4 million hectares, area subject to shifting cultivation reported 4.9 million hectares and riverine and torrents erosion due to floods and eutrophication due to agricultural run off reported 2.7 million hectares. The increasing intensification and extensification also results in salination, alkalisation and water logging in irrigated areas of the country. For achieving and maintaining food security, sustainable forestry agricultural and rural developments controlling of land/soil erosion is very much necessary.

Most part of the applied pesticides and fertilisers, irrespective of crop, applicator or the formulation used, ultimately finds its way into the soil. Before pesticides are completely inactivated, they may adversely affect the functioning of non-target microbes and other forms of life inhabiting the soil. They may also be taken up by the plants or get translocated in the aquatic system by leaching or run-off, thus contaminating the plankton, fish, invertebrate and other forms of life using their water. Pesticide residues in food items have been a matter of considerable concern. Even small quantities of these residues ingested daily along with food can build up high levels in the body fat. The long term effects of these residues in the human body include carcinogenecity, reduced life span and fertility, increased cholesterol, high infant mortality and varied metabolic and genetic disorders.

Traces of pesticides and fertilizers from the fields are washed into the nearest water bodies at the onset on monsoons or whenever there are heavy showers that add to water pollution. Consumers are affected by agricultural concomitants such as pesticides and fertilisers that run-off from fields into rivers. Polluting a river is dangerous because generally, rivers are the primary source of drinking water for towns and cities downstream of the point of pollution. The New Agricultural Policy seeks to sensitise the farming community with the environmental concerns. The policy lays that concerted efforts will be made to pool, distil and evaluate traditional practices, knowledge and wisdom and to harness them for sustainable agricultural growth. The increasing river water pollution is the biggest threat to public health. The diseases commonly caused due to polluted water are cholera, diarrhea, hepatitis, typhoid amoebic and bacillary, dysentery, guinea worm, whereas scabies, leprosy, trachoma and conjucvitis are some of the diseases associated with water scarcity. All these could be attributed to the rapidly increasing population and lack of water resources. Inadequate access to safe drinking water and sanitation facilities leads to higher infant mortality and intestinal diseases. More than one million children died due to diarrhea and other gastrointestinal disorders in 1990s. In addition, around 90 lakh cases of acute diarrhea diseases have been reported in India, Uttar Pradesh reporting the highest number of cases. It is estimated that 73 million workdays are lost every year due to water related diseases. The cost of treating them and the loss in production amount to Rs. 600 crores a year.

9.4. Consumption Distribution

Every cumulative consumption distribution during the eighties and nineties stochastically dominates the previous distribution. The only ambiguity is in 1987-88 where stochastic dominance fails at the 50th per centile vis-à-vis the 1983 distribution. Even this distribution however dominates the 1977-78 one. The consumption distribution has unambiguously improved during the nineties. The anomalies arise because the urban distribution is not unidirectional, dependent as it is on the migration from surrounding rural areas (push and pull factors).

9.4.1. Poverty Trends

There are numerous controversies regarding the measurement of poverty. The most important one relates to the adjustment of individual consumption levels as derived from a survey, by the ratio of the per capita consumption from the National account statistics to the survey mean for the same item. Such an adjustment leaves the distribution of consumption unaffected while changing the calculated poverty rate. Before 1993 such an adjustment was routinely made in calculating poverty rates, after 1993 it has been discontinued. The World Bank's Country Economic Memorandums for India however introduced the change in methodology several years earlier. We were critical of the change in methodology by the World Bank and the Planning Commission and continue to believe that an adjustment of the survey mean is necessary to get a true picture of the poverty rates. The World Bank's series covers the entire period from the 1950s on a consistent basis and is therefore essential for finding out what happened in phase I as well as for comparing poverty in the two phases.

The 3rd order polynomial trend line fitted to the World Bank poverty data shows that poverty increased during the fifties and sixties. This happened despite the fact that per capita GDP grew at a trend rate of between 1% and 2% per annum through out these two decades. The increase in poverty therefore coincided with a declining rate of growth of per capita income and private consumption. Since the early seventies, poverty has been on a clear down trend according to all series. The official poverty calculations based on large sample surveys shows a steeper decline in poverty (especially in the nineties) than the World Bank series. The declining trend in poverty rate therefore coincided with an acceleration in the trend growth of Per capita GDP and TFPG from the mid-1970s.

9.4.2. Poverty Estimates

The most recent controversy regarding poverty estimates relates to the manner in which the data was collected in the 1999-2000 survey. Briefly there are three categories of goods in the consumption surveys: Food products that are purchased frequently (daily/weekly), semi-durable goods that are purchased with moderate frequency (monthly/quarterly) and durable goods that are purchased occasionally (annual/biannual or less). To obtain optimal recall it would be appear to be best to use the 7-day recall period for the first category, 30 day for the second and 365 day for the last. The National sample surveys have been rightly experimenting with these periods, but perhaps without giving due regard to the implications for comparability of poverty estimates over time. In the 1999-2000 survey, for the first time the same set of households were asked to give their food consumption for 7 days and 30 days, thus making it non-comparable with earlier periods when only the 30 day question was asked. It was subsequently discovered that there was another source of non-comparability. The use of the 365-day recall period for a sub-set of commodities in 1999-2000, whereas the 30-day recall was used for these commodities earlier.

9.4.3. Hunger

The FAO defines about 19% of the people in developing countries (828 million) as hungry, while the proportion of Hungry in S. Asia is asserted to be about 20% (254 million). The World food programme on the other hand claims that nearly 50% of the hungry in the World live in India and 35% (350 million) are food insecure.

It is useful to look at these numbers in relation to poverty, because logically the number of hungry people must be a fraction (less than 100%) of the poor for any reasonable definition of poverty. More formally the line defining the 'very poor' or 'hungry' must logically lie below the poverty line. Thus the hunger ratio must be lower that the poverty ratio. The ratio of very poor/hungry to the poor may in general decline, stay constant or rise, depending on the distribution of consumption in the lower half of the distribution. That 18.5 million people went hungry and 260 million people were still poor half a century after Independence is matter of great sadness for the nation.

9.4.4. Life and Literacy

Only a few indicators of health and education are available on a continuous basis and for earlier periods. On the health side Mortality and life expectancy data is available since 1960-61 and on the education side literacy data is available from the same date. This allows us to compare the performance of these over the two phases of growth and to see whether they are consistent with the data on poverty and hunger. The quantity & quality of public and quasi-public goods and services have a have a critical influence on the basic health and education indicators in low income countries. These include public health measures (control of communicable diseases & epidemics), public education (nutrition, personal hygiene, ORT), the supply of clean water, sewerage and sanitation and primary education.

9.4.5. Governance Failure

The constitution enjoined the State to provide education. The courts interpreted these to create a government monopoly over Primary and Secondary education (State list) and degree granting colleges/universities (Central list). The government(s) took 40 years to set up a network of schools, where on average 25% of teachers are absent from school, another 25% are absent from the class, and 5% or more are just sitting in class. Overall the quality of teaching is abysmal, despite teachers getting much higher salary than in the reluctantly permitted, bureaucratically oppressed, non-profit schools. A government monopoly coupled with low accountability and poor governance is the worst possible solution to any economic or social problem. Our constitutionally mandated and court interpreted education system is an approximation of this hypothetical one. The solution is greater accountability (via user groups) to those who are directly affected by this failure, namely the parents and grandparents of school age children. Sustained accountability also requires the involvement of Panchayati Raj institutions and non-govt organisations.

9.5. Poverty Elimination

9.5.1. Cost of Eliminating Poverty

The cost of eliminating poverty and hunger in India of course depends on the extent of poverty, which is currently mired in academic debates about the measurement of poverty. There is however universal agreement that in the years from 1993-94 to 1999-2000 the poverty rate (HCR) was between 25% and 35%.

In 1993-94 the Central government expenditure in the budget category "subsidies" was Rs. 12,682 crore of which Rs. 10,099 crore were for food and fertiliser subsidies. The latter would have been enough to bring all the poor to the consumption level of the person/household at the 25% level. During the same year the Central and State governments together spent another Rs. 14,160 crore on the budget categories 'Rural development,' 'Welfare of SC, ST & OBCs' and 'Social Security and Welfare.' This expenditure would have been enough to bring all the poor to the consumption level of the person/household at the 30% level. These two sets of expenditures (Rs. 25850) would have been more than sufficient to eliminate poverty in 1993 if transferred directly to the poor and disadvantaged (SC, ST, handicapped, old, poor farmers). In 1999-2000 the total subsidies provided by the Central government were Rs. 25,690 crore of which Rs. 22,680 crore were for food and fertiliser.

9.5.2. Income Transfers

It can be argued that the ideal (most efficient) social welfare policy is a direct transfer of income to the poor through a negative income tax. In a developed country this would be very easy. Transfer these amounts directly to the poor, the needy and the disadvantaged in a poor country by setting up an Indian version using a modern smart card system that delivers cash and/or subsidies to the poor based on their entitlements as per specified parameters and norms. Such a smart card could be programmed with identity, and have information on social (SC/ST) and personal/household characteristics.

The entitlement could be varied with and dependent on various economic and social handicaps such as SCST, age (infant or aged), mental handicap, physical disability, female head of household, lactating mother, chronic illness. In this way all the current stakeholders, special interest groups and social policies could be accommodated within a single integrated system. These subsidies would have to be collected by the provider of the specified service from the government through the smart card system just as is done currently in a credit card system. Alternatively all these entitlements could be calculated and consolidated into a single cash value to be delivered to the beneficiary every month at his residential address, through the smart card system. The entitled person would pay the difference between the market price and the subsidy directly to the private or public entity supplying the goods or services.

9.5.3. PDS Non-experiment

If poverty could be eliminated so easily why has this not been tried before? There are many reasons, but the most fundamental is illustrated by the following experience: In the formulation of the tenth Plan as Advisor (Development Policy) responsible for food policy/ PDS system the author proposed the gradual introduction of a credit /debit /smart card system to replace the existing PDS system characterized by enormous leakages and high administrative costs. In this system the entitled person could obtain the specified subsidy from any participating supplier of food/cereals. The person would pay the supplier the difference between the market price and the unit subsidy, and the supplier would collect the subsidy from the government. The formal proposal was to carry out an experiment (as a first step) to determine its effectiveness and to learn about and iron out any problems that may arise. Consequently funds were allocated in the tenth plan for introducing it in a sample of urban areas along with the introduction of food stamp system in a sample of rural areas. Not a single State govt has agreed to undertake this experiment so far, as it has the potential of dramatically reducing leakages and administrative costs.

9.5.4. Smart Card System

The smart card would also constitute a national identity card. For instance the card could contain information on citizenship and voting eligibility (constituency for voting) as provided and checked by the home ministry and the election commission respectively. Secrecy and confidentiality clauses would have to be built into the national smart card system by law. For instance, any person who does not want to avail of any subsidies / entitlements from the government need not provide the information needed for calculating & monitoring the subsidy/entitlement. They would for instance only provide the information necessary to obtain a passport and voter registration card. Many agencies of government have proposed identification cards. There are significant economies of scale in having one smart card system for all citizens, with different agencies having their own special modules within the card for their specialised needs.

The setting up of a smart card system is somewhat distinct from running it even though there may be economies of scope. The former is very similar to carrying out a (special) census in which the data gathered would be entered into a smart card. There is however an additional, technically challenging component, the simultaneous recording of a photo and a biometric fingerprint so as to minimise fraud. The experience with a similar system used in SEBI MAPIN project suggests that it would be best to subcontract it to private parties in each State/region. The running of smart card system is on the other hand very much like the running of a credit card system. All the credit card companies, as well as companies that provide back office services to credit card issuers or marketers, would be interested in competing to obtain the contract for the running of such a system. As a credit card company has to incur a fixed cost in setting up its own credit card system, these companies may be willing to charge below cost if they can share the fixed costs of the public system with their private card systems. This could make a significant difference in the cost of spreading the system to the rural areas. Cash delivery through smart card would be akin to a modern version of the Post & Telegraph department's money order system, already operational with specialised companies that intermediate international/national remittances. The cost of setting up and running a nationwide cash delivery system for the poor would probably be significantly less than that of a commodity related system.

The total steady state cost of running this system should be of the same order as the current credit card systems (< 10%). The identity of the households below the poverty line is not fixed from year to year. The largest turnover occurs because of health shocks followed by natural disasters (droughts and floods) that knock people below the poverty line, while others who have recovered from the shock or have improved their position move above the line. As a matter of abundant caution we could target the bottom half of the population for issue of smart cards (with complete entitlement related information). Annual updating of entitlement related information could be done for those below the poverty line and those up to half this percentage above the line (i.e. if poverty rate, HCR, is 24%, cover poorest 36%).

9.5.5. Regulatory Authority

An independent authority including government officials and non-government organisations could be set up to monitor the integrity of the Poverty Elimination System. This supervisory authority would ensure that private operators are running the smart card system in a manner needed to ensure that the subsidy reaches the poor. Poverty, which rose during the socialist period (1950-1 to 1979-80), has been on a clear down trend during the Market reform period (1980-1 to current). The level of poverty in 1999-2000 is estimated to be between 26.1% and 28.5% as per the Planning Commission methodology. This level of poverty is to be expected in a low income country like India.

9.6. Conclusion

The country's population has multiplied three-fold and the share of rural population has declined whereas the share of urban population has been increased in around five decades. Density has increased more than doubles over the period. The death rates have been declined faster as compared to birth rates but infant mortality is still high. The percentage of people below poverty line declined from 1973 to 1999-2000. Over the period 1987-88 to 1999-2000, urban poverty declined faster as compared to rural poverty.

Rapid population growth has led to the overexploitation of natural resources. The land use pattern in India does not depict substantial changes over period characterised by trends in croplands, pasture lands and forestlands. The deforestation has led to the shrinking of forest cover, which eventually affects human health. However, environmental pollution not only leads to deteriorating environmental conditions but also have adverse effects on the sustainable development and health of people. The considerable amount of both ground water and surface water contamination due to chemical fertilisers and insecticides in the country leads to various water borne diseases.

The creation of employment opportunities is essential in agricultural areas with high poverty, unemployment and landlessness. Poverty also affects the demographic characteristics of the population and hinders the transition to slower population growth. For protecting natural resources and environment, sustainable forestry, rural developments, controlling of water contamination due to chemical fertilisers, pesticides, land/soil erosion, is very much necessary. Special efforts should be made for informing and educating the people and local leaders about the adverse effects of large population through specially designed IEC (Information, Education and Communication) activities. In order to increase green cover and to preserve the existing forests, afforestation and social forestry programmes should be implemented at the local level. More emphasis should be laid on compulsory environmental education at the school level in order to make people aware of the environment protection. The environment protection should not be a responsibility of government alone but local people and leaders should be encouraged to make dedicated efforts to eradicate the environmental problems.

References

Carter Brandon and Kirsten Honmann, "Valuing Environmental Costs in India: The Economy Wide Impact of Environment Degradation", World Bank, mimeo, 1991-92.

Green, C.P., "The Environment and Population Growth: Decade for Action", *Population Reports*, Series M, No. 10, Vol. XX, No. 2, Baltimore, Johns Hopkins School of Public Health, Population Information Program, 1992.

Gulati, S. C., "Population-Development-Environmental Linkages in India", *Paper presented in Millennim Conference on Population,* Development and Environment Nexus organised by IASP, PFI and UNFPA at New Delhi, February 14-16, 2000.

United Nations, "World Population 2000", *United Nations*, Population Division, Department of Economic and Social Affairs, New York, 2001.

WHO, "Our Planet, Our Earth", *Report of the WHO Commission on Health and Environment*, World Health Organization, Geneva, 1992.

10

Demographic Challenges

10.1. Introduction

The demographic reviews major population trends relating to population size and growth, urbanisation and city growth, population ageing, fertility and contraception, mortality, including HIV/AIDS, and international migration. In addition, a section on population policies has been included, in which the concerns and responses of Governments to the major population trends are summarised. The outcomes of the United Nations conferences convened during the 1990s set an ambitious development agenda reaffirmed by the United Nations Millennium Declaration in September 2000. The 1994 International Conference on Population and Development, being one of the major United Nations conferences of the decade, addressed all population aspects relevant for development and provided in its Programme of Action a comprehensive set of measures to achieve the development objectives identified. Given the crucial importance of population factors for development, the full implementation of the Programme of Action and the key actions for its further implementation will significantly contribute to the achievement of the universally agreed development goals, including those in the Millennium Declaration.

The world demographic trends are based on population estimates and projections made separately for each country or area. Projections of the population by age and sex are prepared by using the components method, which requires that explicit assumptions be made about future levels of fertility, mortality and international migration. The monitoring of national population policies at the international level has a long history that goes back to the World Population Plan of Action adopted at the United Nations World Population Conference held in Bucharest in August 1974. The policies examined cover the major population variables and are presented in a descriptive and concise format, focusing on analytical comparisons of countries and regions at present as well as over time. As is the case in the preparation of population estimates and projections, the monitoring of national population policies is guided by principles of objectivity and non-advocacy.

10.2. World Demographic Trends

10.2.1. Population size and Growth

World population passed 6 billion persons at the end of the twentieth century and stands at 6.5 billion in 2005. It is currently growing at 1.2 per cent annually. The addition of the sixth billion took place in a 12-year period, namely, between 1987 and 1999, which is the shortest period within which the world has gained a billion persons. The addition of the next billion, the seventh, is expected to take about 13 years. The population of the world is expected to increase by 2.6 billion during the next 45 years, from 6.5 billion today to 9.1 billion in 2050 (medium variant). However the realisation of these projections is contingent on ensuring that couples have access to family planning and that efforts to arrest the current spread of the HIV/AIDS epidemic are successful in reducing its growth momentum.

The population of the more developed regions, currently estimated at slightly more than 1.2 billion persons, is anticipated to change little during the coming decades. However, some noteworthy demographic changes are expected to occur. In many countries, especially in Europe, populations are projected to decline, as fertility levels are expected to remain below replacement levels. Other developed countries will see their populations continue to grow because their fertility levels are closer to replacement levels and because of significant flows of international migration. The population of the less developed regions is projected to rise steadily, from about 5.3 billion persons today to 7.8 billion persons by mid-century (medium variant). That projection assumes continuing declines in fertility. In the absence of such declines, the population of the less developed regions could be substantially larger than projected. Particularly rapid growth is expected in the group of 50 countries classified as the least developed. By mid-century, for example, the population of the least developed countries could more than double in size.

The annual increment to world population during 2000-2005 has been estimated at 76 million persons. The growth of the United States population represents close to 4 per cent of world population growth; however, about 40 per cent of the population growth of the United States is the result of international migration.

While world population is continuing to grow, considerable diversity exists in the expected population growth of countries. Though it is anticipated that the population of many countries will increase greatly in the coming decades, several countries are expected to grow little and quite a few are actually projected to experience a decline in their population size. India is expected to be the largest contributor to world population growth by far, adding around 570 million persons by 2050.

10.2.2. Urbanisation and City Growth

The world's urban population reached 3.2 billion persons in 2005 and is expected to rise to 5 billion persons by 2030. On the other hand, the rural population of the world is expected to decline slightly from 3.3 billion in 2005 to 3.2 billion in 2030. Whereas 30 per cent of the world population lived in urban areas in 1950, the proportion of urban-dwellers rose to 49 per cent by 2005 and half the world population is expected to live in urban areas by 2007. The world's proportion of urban population is projected to reach 61 per cent in 2030.

The urban population in the more developed countries will be growing at an annual rate of change of only 0.5 per cent. The process of urbanisation is already very advanced in the more developed regions, where 75 per cent of the population lived in urban areas in 2005. Nevertheless, the concentration of population in cities is expected to continue, so that by 2030, 82 per cent of the inhabitants of the more developed countries will be urban-dwellers. The level of urbanisation is considerably lower in the less developed regions, where 43 per cent of the population lived in urban areas in 2005. That proportion is expected to rise to 57 per cent by 2030.

There are marked differences in the level and pace of urbanisation among the major areas constituting the less developed regions of the world. Latin America and the Caribbean as a whole are highly urbanised, with 78 per cent of the population living in urban settlements in 2005, a proportion higher than that of Europe. By 2030, 85 per cent of the population of Latin America and the Caribbean is projected to be urban, a proportion similar to that of Northern America (87 per cent), the most highly urbanised area of the world. With almost 40 per cent of their respective populations living in urban areas in 2005, Africa and Asia are considerably less urbanised, but, are expected to experience rapid rates of urbanisation during the period 2005-2030. It is projected that by 2030, 54 per cent and 55 per cent, respectively, of their inhabitants will live in urban areas.

The proportion of people living in very large urban agglomerations or mega-cities is relatively small. In 2005, 4.5 per cent of the world population resided in cities of 10 million inhabitants or more and by 2015 that proportion is expected to rise to 5 per cent. In contrast, 25 per cent of the world population lived in urban settlements with fewer than 500,000 inhabitants and by 2015 that proportion will likely rise to 27 per cent. In 2005, 39 per cent of the population in the developed countries lived in those small urban settlements; a decade from now, that proportion is expected to be similar at 40 per cent. In the less developed regions, where the majority of the population still resides in rural areas, the proportion of people living in small cities was 22 per cent in 2005 and will rise to 25 per cent by 2015.

10.2.3. Population Ageing

During the twentieth century, the proportion of older persons (those aged 60 years or over) continued to rise and this trend is expected to continue well into the twenty-first century. For example, the proportion of older persons was 8 per cent in 1950 and 10 per cent in 2005 and is projected to reach about 22 per cent by mid-century. The majority of older persons are women, as life expectancy for women is higher than that for men. In 2005, there were 67 million more women than men aged 60 years or over and, at the oldest ages (80 years or above), there were almost twice as many women as men. The declines in fertility reinforced by increasing longevity have produced and will continue to produce unprecedented changes in the age structure of all societies, notably the historic reversal in the proportions of young and older persons. The profound, pervasive and enduring consequences of population ageing present opportunities as well as challenges for all societies.

Globally, the population of older persons is growing by 2.0 per cent each year, considerably faster than the population as a whole. For at least the next 25 years, the older population is expected to continue growing more rapidly than other age groups. The growth rate of those aged 60 years or over will reach 3.1 per cent annually in the period 2010-2015. Such rapid growth will require far-reaching economic and social adjustments in most countries. The population of all countries will continue to age substantially. For example, the median age of the world will rise from 28 years today to 38 years in 2050. As already noted, the number of persons aged 60 years or over will rise from 10 per cent of the world population today to 22 per cent in 2050. The percentage aged 80 years or over will rise from just 1 per cent today to 4 per cent in 2050.

10.3. Population Challenges and Development Goals

Marked differences exist between regions in the number and proportion of older persons. In the more developed regions, one fifth of the population was aged 60 years or over in the year 2005; by 2050, that proportion is expected to reach one third. In the less developed regions, 8 per cent of the population is currently over age 60; however, by 2050, older persons will make up one fifth of the population. As the pace of population ageing is much faster in the developing countries than in the developed ones, developing countries will have less time to adjust to the consequences of population ageing. Moreover, population ageing in the developing countries is taking place at much lower levels of socio-economic development than has been the case in the developed countries. The older population is itself ageing. The fastest-growing age group in the world is the oldest old, those aged 80 years or over. Their number is currently increasing at a rate of 4.2 per cent per year and they constitute more than one eighth of the total number of older persons. By the middle of the century, one fifth of older persons will be aged 80 years or over. The potential support ratio (PSR) (the number of persons aged 15-64 years per one older person aged 65 years or over) indicates the dependency burden on potential workers. The impact of demographic ageing is visible in the PSR, which has fallen and will continue to fall. From 1950 to 2005, the PSR fell from 12 to 9 people in the working ages per each person aged 65 years or over. By mid-century, the PSR for the world is projected to fall to four working-age persons for each person aged 65 years or over. PSRs have important implications for social security schemes, particularly traditional systems in which current workers pay for the benefits of current retirees.

10.3.1. Life Expectancy at Birth

10.3.1.1. Fertility and contraception

Fertility has declined substantially over the last several decades in all areas of the world. Around 30 years ago, for example, the total fertility rate-that is to say, the average number of children a woman would bear if fertility rates remained unchanged during her lifetime-was close to five children per woman at the world level. By the end of the twentieth century, the fertility rate had declined to slightly less than three children per woman. In 2000-2005, 84 countries or areas exhibited fertility levels at or below replacement level. These countries accounted for about 45 per cent of the world's population, or 2.8 billion persons in 2003. Because their levels of fertility are low and are expected to remain low during the coming decades, the populations of those countries are projected to grow relatively little by mid-century, and in a number of countries population is expected to decline.

The remaining countries of the world, with a combined population of about 3.5 billion persons, exhibit total fertility levels above replacement level. Forty-two countries have fertility levels at or above five children per woman in 2000-2005. As a consequence, the population of that group of countries is expected to grow markedly in the coming decades. Among the developing countries, the pace of fertility decline during the recent past has varied significantly. Although by 2000-2005 most countries in the less developed regions are already far advanced in the transition from high to low fertility, there are some 13 countries that exhibit sustained high fertility and for which either there is no recent evidence about fertility trends or the available evidence does not indicate the onset of sustained fertility decline. In those countries, even though fertility is projected to decline after 2005, it is not expected to reach replacement level by the period 2045-2050. The high fertility of those countries will lead to rapid population growth. All but the Congo belong to the group of the least developed countries. The continuation of rapid population growth presents serious challenges to the future development of those countries.

Contraceptive use increased markedly over the past decade. At the global level, contraceptive prevalence increased from 54 per cent in 1990 to 59 per cent in 1995 and to an estimated 63 per cent in 2000. The fastest increases were in Africa and Latin America and the Caribbean where contraceptive prevalence increased by more than 1 percentage point per year, on average. The increase was less rapid in Asia where prevalence increased by 0.8 percentage points per year between 1990 and 2000. Modern methods account for a large proportion of current contraceptive use, especially in the less developed regions where they account for 90 per cent of contraceptive use compared with 81 per cent in the more developed regions. The three methods most used are female sterilisation, the intrauterine device (IUD) and the pill, with prevalence levels of 21 per cent, 14 per cent and 7 per cent, respectively. These three methods account for two thirds of use worldwide.

Traditional methods are more popular in the developed countries than in the developing countries: they are used by 13 per cent of married couples in the more developed countries compared with just 6 per cent in the developing countries. The most used traditional methods include rhythm (periodic abstinence) and withdrawal. In the world as a whole, those methods are used by about 7 per cent of married women. Short-acting and reversible methods are more popular in the developed countries, whereas longer-acting methods are more popular in the developing countries. In the developed countries, contraceptive users rely mostly on pills (16 per cent of married women) and condoms (13 per cent). In contrast, female sterilisation and IUDs, used by 23 per cent and 15 per cent of married women, respectively, dominate in the developing countries.

10.3.1.2. Mortality, including HIV/AIDS

During the twentieth century, mortality experienced the most rapid decline in the history of humanity. Although the sustained reduction of mortality had started in the eighteenth century, it gained momentum in the early part of the twentieth century as better hygiene, improved nutrition and medical practices based on scientific evidence became the rule in the more advanced countries. Despite the setbacks brought about by the First and Second World Wars, by the period 1950-1955, mortality had declined markedly in the more developed regions. For example, by the middle of the twentieth century, average life expectancy at birth had reached 66 years, ranging from 63 years in Southern Europe to 70 years in Australia and New Zealand.

The century also marked an important turning point in the less developed regions. With the expanded use of antibiotics, vaccines and insecticides, mortality in the developing world began to decline rapidly. For example, life expectancy at birth for the less developed regions increased by slightly more than 50 per cent from 1950-1955 to 2000-2005, rising from about 41 to 63 years. As a result, the mortality differentials between the less developed and the more developed regions narrowed. By the period 2000-2005, the difference in life expectancy between the two groups amounted to 12 years instead of 25 years, the difference observed in the period 1950-1955.

There remains, however, a group of countries-the least developed-where the reduction of mortality has lagged behind. While mortality declined in the least developed countries, it did not keep pace with mortality improvements in the less developed regions. For example, the difference between the life expectancy for the least developed countries and that for the less developed regions as a whole increased from 5 years in the period 1950-1955 to 12 years in the period 2000-2005. A major reason for such an increase is that the 50 countries classified as least developed include 26 that are highly affected by the HIV/AIDS epidemic.

Until fairly recently it was expected that mortality would continue declining in all countries, especially in those that were still experiencing moderate to high mortality levels because of their late start in the transition to low mortality. However, two developments have made it necessary to adjust those expectations: HIV/AIDS and the shocks from socio-economic transformations in countries with economies in transition. The emergence of the virus that causes acquired immunodeficiency syndrome (AIDS) and the worldwide pandemic that it has generated have already produced marked increases in mortality in the countries most affected by the disease. It is estimated that by the end of 2003, about 58 million persons had been infected by the virus and about 38 million were still alive. Some 92 per cent of those infected with HIV are living in the developing countries, with sub-Saharan Africa experiencing the highest prevalence rates. In addition, the number of countries where HIV prevalence has become significant has been growing rapidly in Asia and Latin America and the Caribbean. While it is not yet certain that the spread in those regions will follow the pattern observed in Africa, rapid and effective responses may be required to avert the devastation that Africa is already experiencing.

It has also become evident that mortality has tended to stagnate or even to increase in certain countries with economies in transition, most of which exhibited fairly low mortality in the period 1950-1955. The causes for the slowdown or reversal of the transition to low mortality are multiple and complex, but they have no doubt been exacerbated by the momentous social and economic transformations resulting from the political changes taking place in the former communist countries since 1985. As a result of those developments and in the light of the increases in mortality that have occurred in countries affected by conflict or civil strife, considerable uncertainty exists about the future path of mortality. It seems less certain than a decade or two ago that mortality will necessarily decrease in all countries in future. Nevertheless, mortality has declined more rapidly than expected in a number of developed countries, so that the possibility of further medical and technological breakthroughs that may increase the human lifespan cannot be ruled out, opening up the prospect of a future where expectations of life at birth of above 85 or 90 years will be a reality in certain populations.

With regard to gender differences in mortality, by the end of the twentieth century, female life expectancy was higher than male life expectancy in all regions, although the difference between the two was relatively small in Western Africa and South-central Asia. However, even in those regions, there was a marked gain in life expectancy for females in relation to males. In the period 1950-1955, South-central Asia had been the only region where females had a lower life expectancy than males.

Female life expectancy increased more than male life expectancy during the last half-century in three major areas: Asia, Europe and Latin America and the Caribbean. In contrast, in Africa, Northern America and Oceania, the female advantage remained relatively unchanged or declined. In Europe, life expectancy of females made the greatest gains with respect to that of males, whereas in Africa life expectancy of males made the greatest gains with respect to that of females. Generally, the female advantage in life expectancy increased from 1950-1955 to 2000-2005.

Over the past half century, a major part of the reduction of mortality has occurred in childhood. Overall levels of life expectancy are strongly determined by mortality at young ages, especially when mortality is high. Consequently, the marked increases in life expectancy that have occurred since 1950 at the world level reflect in large part sharp drops of mortality in childhood. Future reductions of mortality are expected to result in the virtual elimination of deaths at young ages in many countries. However, certain regions and countries are expected to fare better than others in achieving such a goal.

Most regions of the world are projected to see continuing improvements in their mortality rates and, as a result, an increase in their expectations of life to levels that were, until recently, unprecedented in human history. However, for the least developed countries, even the substantial improvements expected by mid-century are unlikely to eliminate the gap in respect of mortality existing between them and the rest of the world. Moreover, given the setbacks that have occurred recently in many of those countries, it may not be at all certain that the projected improvements will be achieved.

10.3.2. International Migration

About 175 million persons, representing about 3 per cent of the world population in 2000, resided in a country other than the one in which they had been born. The number of migrants more than doubled between 1960 and 2000. Sixty per cent of the world's migrants reside in the more developed regions, while 40 per cent reside in the less developed regions. Most of the world's migrants live in Europe (56 million), Asia (50 million) and Northern America (41 million).

In 2000, females constituted almost 49 per cent of all migrants, up from 47 per cent in 1960. While women and girls were slightly more numerous than males among migrants in 2000 in the more developed regions, they accounted for just under 45 per cent of all migrants in the less developed regions. At the regional level, female migrants are more numerous than male migrants in Europe, Latin America and the Caribbean, Northern America and Oceania, but remain underrepresented in many parts of Africa and Asia.

Between 1995 and 2000, the more developed regions of the world gained nearly 13 million migrants from the less developed regions, around 2.6 million migrants per year. Net migration accounted for two thirds of the population growth in the more developed regions. The largest gains took place in Northern America, which absorbed about 1.4 million migrants annually, followed by Europe with an annual net gain of over 1 million.

At the end of 2003, the number of refugees in the world stood at 15 million, of whom approximately 10 million were under the mandate of the Office of the United Nations High Commissioner for Refugees (UNHCR) and 5 million under the mandate of the United Nations Relief and Works Agency for Palestine Refugees in the Near East. The largest numbers of refugees were found in Asia (8 million) and in Africa (3 million). Three million refugees were in the developed countries and 12 million in the developing countries. The remittances sent back to the home country by migrants represent an important aspect of international migration. Those moneys are a major source of foreign exchange earnings for some countries and an important addition to gross domestic product (GDP).

10.3.3. Population Policies

Continued high rates of population growth remain an issue of policy concern for many countries of the developing world. About half of the countries in the less developed regions consider their rate of population growth to be too high. The proportion of such countries encompass much of Africa (77 per cent) and the proportion is significant in Oceania (56 per cent). Concern with rapid population growth is lower among the countries of Asia (36 per cent) and Latin America and the Caribbean (36 per cent).

Nearly 60 per cent of the countries in the less developed regions consider fertility too high and, in the group of 50 least developed countries, close to 80 per cent report fertility as too high. The latter proportion has been rising steadily since the mid-1970s. At that time, about 1 out of 3 of the least developed countries thought its fertility was too high. Adolescent fertility is also a concern for Governments, particularly in the less developed regions. Almost two thirds of the countries in those regions and one third of the countries in the more developed regions view this as a major concern.

Government support for policies and programmes that affect fertility has increased steadily during the last quarter-century: about 90 per cent of countries provide either direct or indirect support for family planning programmes and contraceptives. The practice of limiting access to contraceptives has nearly vanished. Low fertility has become a concern for an increasing number of countries in recent years, particularly in more developed regions. More than half the countries in those regions consider fertility to be too low, up from one fifth in the mid-1970s. Of the 39 countries that consider fertility too low, 27 were in Europe and 9 in Asia. Governments' views of their country's mortality level are split according to development level. About 70 per cent of the countries in the more developed regions consider the level of life expectancy to be acceptable, compared with 35 per cent of the less developed countries and 4 per cent of the least developed countries. Some segments of the population-most notably infants and children under age 5-continue to register unacceptably high mortality levels and are considered problem groups for many countries. Maternal mortality is another serious concern, particularly in the less developed countries. In the less developed regions, 1 country in 5 reports the level of maternal mortality to be acceptable, as compared with three fourths of the countries in the more developed regions. During the 20 years since HIV/AIDS was identified as a disease, the pandemic has emerged as one of the leading causes of adult mortality in many countries, particularly in the less developed regions of the world. More than 80 per cent of the countries in those regions have reported that AIDS is a major concern, as have nearly 90 per cent of the least developed countries. Concern has also been substantial in the more developed regions, where three quarters of the countries view AIDS as a major concern.

Developed and developing countries show a similar inclination towards restricting immigration. Among developed and developing countries, one third have policies aimed at lowering their immigration levels. In comparison, in the mid-1970s, 18 per cent of the developed countries and 3 per cent of the developing countries had adopted such policies. Concerning emigration, both the developed and the developing countries show similar trends in their views and policies. About 3 out of 4 countries, whether developed or developing, view their level of emigration as satisfactory, whereas 1 country in 4 has policies aimed at lowering emigration. For many years, Governments have expressed concern about the spatial distribution of their populations. This concern often arises from high levels of migration from rural to urban areas, urban sprawl and the uncontrolled growth of primate cities and metropolitan areas. Governments in the past have attempted to change distribution in a variety of ways, inter alia, through building new capitals, encouraging growth in small and medium-sized cities rather than in large ones, creating regional development zones, controlling the movement of people to cities and limiting urban sprawl by curbing development. Most of those attempts have failed to achieve their objectives, and population distribution remains an area of major concern to a significant number of Governments, particularly in the less developed regions.

10.3.3.1. Achieving development goals

The goal of development is to improve the quality of life of all people. In that sense, population is at the core of development. In 2005, 759 million, or 12 per cent, of the 6.5 billion inhabitants of the world live in the least developed countries. Between 2005 and 2015, the least developed countries as a whole are expected to absorb a quarter of all population growth in the world. High fertility levels characterise the majority of the least developed countries. Consequently, their populations are still young, with 42 per cent of their inhabitants being children under age 15. Levels of extreme poverty in most of the least developed countries are high: over 20 per cent of their overall population live in extreme poverty, surviving on less than US$ 1 per day, and in 10 of them that proportion is higher than 40 per cent. Although fertility levels have started to decline in some of the least developed countries, the desired number of children remains high. Nevertheless, in the majority of the least developed countries, the number of children that women have surpasses the number desired, suggesting that universal provision of family planning services could result in a reduction of unwanted fertility.

Most countries of Latin America and the Caribbean are already far advanced in the transition to low fertility. Average fertility in the region is currently 2.5 children per woman. Children under age 15 account for 30 per cent of the population and persons aged 65 years or over account for 6 per cent. There are about 6 dependants (children and the elderly) per every 10 adults of working age and that ratio is expected to continue declining as fertility falls even further. Although levels of extreme poverty tend to be below 10 per cent in most of Latin America and the Caribbean, countries in Central America tend to have higher levels of extreme poverty and most Latin American countries are characterised by the prevalence of very unequal income distributions.

A major concern in the region is therefore the reduction of this inequality. Population trends vary considerably in the remaining developing countries, with current fertility ranging from less than 1.5 children per woman in Armenia, Georgia and the Republic of Korea to over 5 children per woman in the Congo and Nigeria. On average, these countries have a fertility of about 3.1 children per woman, higher than that in Latin America and the Caribbean but similar to that of India. Because of their higher average fertility, the proportion of children in their population stands at 33 per cent, whereas the proportion of elderly amounts to just 5 per cent. The number of dependants per 10 adults of working age is 6, lower than the equivalent value of 8 for the least developed countries. That is, just as the latter would, the higher-fertility countries in this group would most likely benefit from increased efforts to reduce unwanted fertility. The countries in this group located in sub-Saharan Africa tend to have high levels of extreme poverty, often surpassing 20 per cent. Levels of extreme poverty tend to be lower in the Asian and North African countries in this group. In developed countries, fertility declined much earlier than in the developing world and has been very low since the 1980s. Consequently, population declined in 17 developed countries during 2000-2005 and during 2005-2015 will do so in 25 of them, including Italy, the Russian Federation and Ukraine. Furthermore, population ageing is more advanced in developed countries, where over 15 per cent of the population is aged 65 years or over and just 17 per cent is under age 15. The dependency ratio in the developed world is currently under 5 children and elderly persons per 10 adults of working age but it is rising and is expected to reach 7 by 2050.

Rising dependency ratios are also expected in China over the next 40 years but not in India, Latin America and the Caribbean and the rest of the developing world taken as a whole. In all groups and regions, however, the proportion of elderly is expected to rise as the proportion of children falls with declining fertility. The expected reductions in fertility are consistent with the continued implementation of the Programme of Action of the International Conference on Population and Development and would be less likely to materialise in certain regions if the objective of providing family planning services to all who needed and wanted them was not met. The world today encompasses, therefore, countries at all stages of the demographic transition, that is to say, the transition from a regime of high fertility and high mortality producing low population growth to one where both fertility and mortality are low and produce again low rates of population change. The fact that, during the transition, mortality reductions usually precede fertility reductions leads to a period of rapid population growth. The end of that period of rapid growth has been reached or is within reach of about two fifths of humanity today. Another two fifths of the world population is already advanced on the path to lower population growth, but the remaining fifth is still growing very rapidly, largely because it has barely begun the transition to low fertility. Furthermore, for all the countries that are highly affected by the HIV/AIDS epidemic, the transition to lower mortality has been interrupted, and the epidemic is having major detrimental effects on both population trends and socio-economic development. Bearing this context in mind is therefore crucial in assessing to what extent the implementation of the Programme of Action can contribute to the achievement of the agreed development goals, since its recommendations for action are not equally relevant for all countries.

10.3.4. Importance of Human Rights

Respect for human rights underpins the attainment of development because if a person's human rights are not safeguarded and respected that person's well-being is undermined. A number of objectives and recommendations contained in the Programme of Action are justifiable not only because they lead to development or have positive impacts on the socio-economic status of people, but because they are an expression of the fundamental rights of the individual.

A key aspect of the Programme of Action is its emphasis on measures to advance gender equality and equity and the empowerment of women as a matter of right. As with education, this goal is important in itself and need not be justified in terms of its likely impact on development. The Programme of Action underscores that the "human rights of women and the girl child are an inalienable, integral and indivisible part of universal human rights". Such recognition is also reflected in the Millennium Development Goal of promoting gender equality and the empowerment of women. In sum, implementing the Programme of Action in all its aspects would not only contribute to the attainment of a number of universally agreed development goals but also ensure that all people enjoy fully certain key human rights.

10.3.5. Achieving Sustainable Development

The key development goal for the international community is to achieve sustainable development as a means to ensure human well-being, equitably shared by all people today and in the future.

The Programme of Action also has this as an overriding goal. According to the Programme of Action, the achievement of sustainable development requires that the interrelationships between population, resources, the environment and development be fully recognised, properly managed and brought into a harmonious, dynamic balance. Because population is expected to increase substantially, especially in developing countries, the Programme of Action recognises the usefulness of achieving a lower population growth as early as possible. It notes that in many countries, slower population growth has bought more time to adjust to future population increases, improving the ability of those countries to combat poverty, protect and repair the environment, and set the conditions for sustainable development. Even the difference of a single decade in the transition to stabilisation levels of fertility can have a considerable positive impact on quality of life. Consequently, the Programme of Action calls for the formulation of development strategies that realistically reflect the short-term, medium-term and long-term implications of population dynamics by integrating population into development and environment programmes that take into account patterns of production and consumption and seek to bring about population trends consistent with the achievement of sustainable development and the improvement of the quality of life.

The Programme of Action notes that, to ensure the economic well-being of growing populations, investment in human resource development must be given priority, by increasing access to, inter alia, information, education, skill development and employment opportunities. It particularly underscores that existing inequities and barriers to women in the workforce should be eliminated and that women's access to productive resources, and ownership of land, and their right to inherit property, should be promoted and strengthened. It encourages Governments and the private sector to foster job creation in all sectors by expanding trade and investment on an environmentally sound basis, increasing investment in human resource development, and developing democratic institutions and good governance. Full implementation of these measures would contribute significantly to promoting development.

One of the major development goals is to ensure environmental sustainability, particularly by integrating the principles of sustainable development into country policies and programmes, so as to reverse the loss of environmental resources. The Programme of Action recognises that meeting the basic human needs of growing populations is dependent on a healthy environment and it provides guidance on how to address the human dimensions of pressures on the environment. However, it also recognises that "(d)emographic factors, combined with poverty and lack of access to resources in some areas, and excessive consumption and wasteful production patterns in others, cause or exacerbate problems of environmental degradation and resource depletion and thus inhibit sustainable development". To prevent or reverse these outcomes, the Programme of Action supports the objectives and actions agreed to in Agenda 2116 and recommends that Governments "(i)mplement policies to address the ecological implications of inevitable future increases in population numbers and changes in concentration and distribution, particularly in ecologically vulnerable areas and urban agglomerations". This recommendation, in conjunction with the call for the integration of "demographic factors into environment impact assessments and other planning and decision-making processes aimed at achieving sustainable development", is fully consistent with the Millennium Development Goals and underscores the importance of population aspects in the pursuit of sustainable development. In this regard, although the Programme of Action recognises that further increases in population numbers are inevitable, particularly in the poorer and most vulnerable countries, the implementation of its call for universal access to family planning services is expected to contribute to a reduction in the growth of the world's population.

10.3.5.1. Eradication of poverty

The Programme of Action recognises that "widespread poverty remains the major challenge to development efforts. Poverty is often accompanied by unemployment, malnutrition, illiteracy, low status of women, exposure to environmental risks and limited access to social and health services ... including family planning. All these factors contribute to high levels of fertility, morbidity and mortality, as well as to low economic productivity. Poverty is also closely related to inappropriate spatial distribution of population, to unsustainable use and inequitable distribution of such natural resources as land and water, and to serious environmental degradation". The Programme of Action stresses that sustained economic growth in the context of sustainable development is essential to eradicating poverty, which in turn will contribute to slowing population growth and to achieving early population stabilisation.

In addition, research carried out during the 1990s has shown that changes in the age distribution of a population resulting from declining fertility can help accelerate economic growth. As fertility declines, the proportion of the population comprising children (persons under age 15) also declines, whereas the proportion of the population of working age increases, resulting in a decreasing dependency ratio (defined as the average number of children and elderly persons per 10 persons of working age). Provided jobs are available for the rising number of workers, a country can reap the benefits of increased production and lower costs associated with the decreasing proportion of dependants. This so-called demographic bonus can thus contribute significantly to economic growth and poverty reduction in contexts where governance facilitates human resource development and employment creation. The experience of the newly industrialising countries in Asia provides an example of this outcome. However, over the long run, the demographic bonus dissipates as the population continues to age and the dependency ratio rises again because of increasing proportions of elderly persons.

Implementation of the Programme of Action, particularly of measures to ensure that family planning services are affordable, acceptable and accessible to all who need and want them, can help reduce unwanted fertility, especially in the high-fertility countries of today, and thus trigger the process that gives rise to the demographic bonus. Because most of those high-fertility countries are among the least developed countries where levels of extreme poverty are high, the advantages that can be brought by the demographic bonus can also contribute to the reduction of poverty. However, realising those advantages requires that economic growth be possible in the countries involved and that it be accompanied by substantial job growth. Not all countries experiencing a decline of fertility have seen economic growth increase markedly as a result of the demographic bonus. Many of the countries in Latin America, for instance, have experienced slow economic growth despite being fairly advanced in the transition to low fertility. Most of them are middle-income countries where levels of extreme poverty are low. Relative poverty, however, is significant.

Consequently, in addition to the positive effects that the demographic bonus might still have on economic growth, measures adopted to improve income distribution-for instance, income-generation and employment strategies directed to the poor, as suggested by the Programme of Action-would be of benefit to these countries. The Programme of Action also recognises that high priority should be given "to meeting the needs, and increasing the opportunities, for information, education, jobs, skill development and relevant reproductive health services, of all underserved members of society", who generally include the poor in both urban and rural areas. Its full implementation would therefore contribute to the reduction of inequalities within societies.

Implementation of the Programme of Action can also contribute to the reduction of poverty by preventing pregnancy among young adolescents, reducing maternalmortality, and slowing the spread of HIV. Single adolescent women who become pregnant are more likely to drop out of school, thus compromising their future earning capacity and becoming more likely to end in poverty. Maternal mortality and the mortality of parents due to HIV/AIDS often lead to or exacerbate poverty. The Programme of Action also acknowledges that international migration can have significant positive impacts on development, especially through remittances. Remittances have become the second largest source of foreign exchange for developing countries, following foreign direct investment (FDI). Furthermore, remittance levels are double those of official development assistance (ODA). Remittances benefit both the families that receive them and their communities through multiplier effects and may therefore contribute to the reduction of extreme poverty even if the very poor do not migrate.

10.3.5.2. Reduction of hunger

Because poverty and malnutrition often go together, sustained economic growth broadly shared is also necessary to reduce hunger, particularly in the least developed countries. The Programme of Action acknowledges the importance of attaining food security at all levels and calls for measures to strengthen food, nutrition and agricultural policies and programmes, and fair trade relations. The Millennium Development Goal target of reducing by half, between 1990 and 2015, the proportion of people suffering from hunger is consistent with this call. Because there is no shortage of food worldwide, combating hunger implies providing people with the means of acquiring food. Fair trade is necessary to achieve this objective, since agricultural subsidies in developed countries distort world prices and hurt farmers in developing countries, thereby contributing to high rural poverty in the latter. In sub-Saharan Africa, where population growth has surpassed increases in agricultural productivity, food availability per capita has dropped, leading to rises in malnutrition and hunger. In that region, increases in agricultural productivity, reductions in population growth, improved governance and economic growth would together serve to reduce poverty and hunger.

Implementation of other recommendations in the Programme of Action-including improvements in education and gender equality, the achievement of better child health, the implementation of policies to address the impact of HIV/AIDS and urban poverty, and the provision of reproductive health services that reduce both unwanted fertility and maternal mortality-can also contribute to reducing hunger. Studies have shown that a mother's low educational attainment is the factor most consistently related to malnutrition among children in developing countries. With more education, as called for in the Programme of Action, women are better able to ensure the health and proper nutrition of their children. Enhancing the status of women, particularly by providing them with access to income and resources, can also result in better intra-household distribution of food, thus preventing female malnutrition. Lastly, measures to prevent the spread of HIV are crucial in forestalling the potentially devastating effects that the HIV/AIDS epidemic, by debilitating or reducing the agricultural labour force, can have on agricultural productivity.

10.3.6. Achievement of Universal Primary Education

Improving educational attainment, particularly of girls, would also have an impact on population dynamics, since education is known to influence demographic behaviour with respect to nuptiality, fertility, health and migration. Education also affects the intergenerational formation of human capital, with the education of mothers influencing the educational attainment of children. Conversely, high fertility and rapid population growth have hindered the achievement of universal primary education in many developing countries, especially the least developed. Early marriage and pregnancy among adolescent women often curtail their education. Implementation of the Programme of Action, by preventing early marriage and pregnancy as well as unwanted births, would contribute to achieving universal primary education.

10.3.7. Gender Equality and the Empowerment of Women

Both the Programme of Action and the United Nations Millennium Declaration call for the achievement of gender equality and the empowerment of women, recognising that both are important in combating poverty, hunger and disease and in achieving sustainable development. However, the Programme of Action sets a broader agenda and provides more detailed guidance on how to achieve that goal, not only focusing on measures to improve the status of women but also including recommendations on the involvement and participation of men in realising gender equality. With regard to women, the Programme of Action stresses the importance of increasing their equal participation and equitable representation at all levels of the political process; of improving their ability to earn income in occupations beyond the range of traditional ones so as to achieve economic self-reliance; and of ensuring their equal access to the labour market and social security systems; of ensuring their equal rights to buy, hold and sell property and land, obtain credit and negotiate contracts in their own name, and exercise their right to inheritance. The Programme of Action also underscores the need to eliminate all practices that discriminate against women and all forms of violence against women or girls.

Furthermore, it points out repeatedly that actions to enhance the welfare of people should be particularly tailored to meeting the needs of women and girls. With respect to education, the Programme of Action states that "(e)ducation is one of the most important means of empowering women with the knowledge, skills and self-confidence necessary to participate fully in the development process". It therefore urges countries to ensure the widest and earliest possible access of girls and women to secondary and higher levels of education, as well as to vocational education and technical training. It also calls for the closing of the gender gap in primary and secondary education by 2005, providing guidelines on measures to keep girls and adolescents in school. Its implementation would therefore result in the elimination of gender disparities in primary and secondary education as called for by the Millennium Development Goals.

Acknowledging that "full participation and partnership of both women and men are required in productive and reproductive life, including shared responsibilities for the care and nurturing of children and maintenance of the household", the Programme of Action puts considerable emphasis on the gender aspects of reproductive life, especially in relation to the maintenance of reproductive health and access to reproductive health-care services, including family planning. For women, having access to affordable, acceptable and convenient reproductive health-care services is essential to having control over their reproductive lives and to ensuring that the timing of their pregnancies fits with their family, education and work plans. Realising the reproductive rights of women is therefore essential for their empowerment. However, according to the objectives stressed by the Programme of Action, both women and men should "have access to the information, education and services needed to achieve good sexual health and exercise their reproductive rights and responsibilities" and it is also important "to emphasise men's shared responsibility and promote their active involvement in responsible parenthood, sexual and reproductive behaviour, including family planning; prenatal, maternal and child health; prevention of sexually transmitted diseases, including HIV; prevention of unwanted and high-risk pregnancies; shared control and contribution to family income, children's education, health and nutrition; and recognition and promotion of the equal value of children of both sexes."

In essence, full implementation of the Programme of Action entails both the empowerment of women in all spheres of life and a greater involvement of men in the exercise of reproductive rights and responsibilities. The achievement of gender equality in those terms would not only be consistent with the improvement of the status of women as called for in the Beijing Platform for Action, but also contribute to enhancing economic growth and reducing poverty through the growing and more productive participation of women in the economy; to reducing child mortality and improving maternal health because of the increasing education and decision-making power of women; and to reducing the transmission of HIV by improving the willingness of men and women to accept responsibility for their own and their partner's sexual health.

10.3.8. Improvement of Health

Good health is essential for the well-being of individuals and societies. In countries where poor health is common, labour productivity suffers. High rates of morbidity and mortality are still common in many low-income countries, especially those highly affected by infectious diseases such as HIV/AIDS, malaria and tuberculosis. A major goal of the international community is to provide access to primary health-care services to all and to reduce the risks of contracting the major infectious diseases. The Programme of Action calls upon all countries to provide primary health care to all and to make efforts to ensure a longer and healthier life for their populations. It sets quantitative goals urging high-mortality countries to achieve a life expectancy at birth greater than 70 years by 2015 and the rest to achieve a life expectancy at birth greater than 75 years by the same date. Achievement of those goals would imply that major progress had been made in combating the major causes of death in poor countries and in providing adequate sanitation and health services to most people on the planet. The full implementation of the Programme of Action would ensure access to health-care services for all people and especially for the most underserved and vulnerable groups.

10.3.9. Reducing Mortality in Childhood

The Programme of Action urged that by 2000, under-five mortality should be reduced by one third or to a maximum of 70 deaths per 1,000 births in all countries, and that under-five mortality should decline to below 45 deaths per 1,000 births in all countries by 2015, a goal consistent with the United Nations Millennium Declaration's goal of reducing under-five mortality by two thirds between 1990 and 2015. The measures proposed to achieve this goal are summarised in the key actions for the further implementation of the Programme of Action as follows: Governments should continue to support reductions in child mortality "by strengthening infant and child health programmes that emphasise improved prenatal care and nutrition, including breastfeeding, unless it is medically contraindicated, universal immunisation, oral rehydration therapies, clean water sources, infectious disease prevention, reduction of exposure to toxic substances, and improvements in household sanitation; and by strengthening maternal health services, quality family-planning services to help couples to time and space births, and efforts to prevent transmission of HIV/AIDS and other sexually transmitted diseases". Clearly, implementation of these measures would contribute to the attainment of the goals set.

Other measures included in the Programme of Action whose implementation would also contribute to the reduction of child mortality are: the reduction of poverty; the increase of educational attainment, especially among women; the improvement of maternal health; the promotion of the empowerment and equality of women; and the reduction of the spread of HIV/AIDS. These measures, which are consistent with several of the goals contained in the United Nations Millennium Declaration, illustrate the synergies existing between the mutually reinforcing development goals and actions recommended by the Programme of Action.

10.3.10. Improving Maternal Health

The Programme of Action calls for an expansion of "the provision of maternal health services in the context of primary health care. These services, based on the concept of informed choice, should include education on safe motherhood, prenatal care that is focused and effective, maternal nutrition programmes, adequate delivery assistance that avoids excessive recourse to Caesarean sections and provides for obstetric emergencies; referral services for pregnancy, childbirth and abortion complications; post-natal care; and family planning. All births should be assisted by trained persons, preferably nurses and midwives, but at least by trained birth attendants". In addition, the Programme of Action urges countries to reduce maternal mortality by one half between 1990 and 2000, and by a further one half by 2015. This goal is equivalent to that of reducing the maternal mortality ratio by 75 per cent between 1990 and 2015 as called for by the United Nations Millennium Declaration, that is to say, implementation of the Programme of Action would fulfil the Millennium Declaration goal.

A key preventive measure to reduce a woman's lifetime probability of dying from pregnancy-related causes is to ensure access to family planning to avoid unwanted pregnancies. In addition, the presence of a trained attendant at delivery and access to emergency obstetric care are essential to preventing deaths occurring because of complications during delivery. Providing access to quality services for the management of complications arising from abortion and offering post-abortion counselling, education and family planning services so as to help prevent repeat abortions are also measures needed to reduce the risks of maternal death.

The achievement of lower maternal mortality, particularly among the vulnerable and underserved population groups, would improve not only the health of women, but also that of their children, and the well-being of their families, thus contributing to reducing child mortality and malnutrition.

10.3.11. Combating HIV/AIDS, Malaria and other Diseases

The Programme of Action recognises that infectious and parasitic diseases continue to be a major affliction of large numbers of people. To combat them, it suggests that developing countries be assisted in producing generic drugs for their domestic markets so as to ensure the wide availability and accessibility of such drugs. This recommendation is complementary to the call in the United Nations Millennium Declaration for the pharmaceutical industry to make essential drugs more widely available to and affordable by all who need them in developing countries. In addition, the Programme of Action calls upon all countries to ensure "a safe and sanitary living environment for all population groups through measures aimed at avoiding crowded housing conditions, reducing air pollution, ensuring access to clean water and sanitation, improving waste management, and increasing the safety of the workplace". Although no explicit mention is made of the provision of insecticide treated netting to protect humans against the bite of the mosquito that transmits malaria, such measures would also be necessary to combat the spread of that disease. Both access to adequate treatment and the implementation of preventive measures to avoid infection are necessary in order to reduce the spread of diseases such as malaria and tuberculosis, and implementation of the Programme of Action would contribute towards making this a reality.

With respect to HIV/AIDS, the Programme of Action underscores the disastrous consequences of the epidemic for individuals, communities and entire nations. It therefore emphasises the need for measures to prevent the spread of HIV and to treat and support those infected. One of its objectives is therefore "(t)o ensure that HIV-infected individuals have adequate medical care and are not discriminated against; to provide counselling and other support for people infected with HIV and to alleviate the suffering of people living with AIDS and that of their family members, especially orphans; to ensure that the individual rights and the confidentiality of persons infected with HIV are respected; and to ensure that sexual and reproductive health programmes address HIV infection and AIDS". This objective, if achieved, would palliate the negative effects of the disease.

The Programme of Action stresses the importance of providing young people and adolescents of both sexes with the information and education needed to prevent the transmission of sexually transmitted diseases, and the need to ensure that adolescent and adult men take responsibility for their own sexual health and the prevention of sexually transmitted diseases. Full implementation of these measures, together with the provisions aimed at improving the status of women and empowering them, would greatly contribute to reducing the transmission of HIV in contexts where the subordination of women to men and the weak economic position of women have constituted a factor promoting the spread of the disease, particularly among women.

10.4. Challenges of Changing Population

10.4.1. Improving Livelihoods

Over the next 15 years, the growth in the world population will be absorbed mainly by urban areas of developing countries, and the world's population will become more urban than rural. As a result, extreme poverty, which has until now been more common in rural than in urban areas, will become increasingly an urban phenomenon. In most developing countries, where urban-dwellers have better access to education and health services than do rural inhabitants, rural-urban migration is a means of improving the access of migrants to such services and of improving their livelihoods. Nevertheless, the rapid pace of urbanisation has strained the capacity of Governments to provide adequate services to urban-dwellers and the number of persons living in slums has been rising, amounting to about 900 million today. In this light, the goal of improving the lives of 100 million slum-dwellers by 2020, one of the goals set forth in the United Nations Millennium Declaration, is a modest one.

Although not all slum-dwellers are poor, those having the greatest needs are among the poor and underserved populations focused on by the Programme of Action when it stresses the importance of providing underserved groups with "information, education, jobs, skill development and reproductive health services". To achieve improvement of the lives of slum-dwellers, programmes aimed specifically at improving their access to basic services are necessary. The Programme of Action provides guidance on the types of improvements required and, implicitly, recognises the importance of targeting programmes to satisfy the particular needs of underserved population groups.

10.4.2. Developing a Global Partnership for Development

The Programme of Action gives considerable attention to the ways and means by which its recommendations may be implemented. In particular, it includes cost estimates for the major components of basic national programmes on population and reproductive health, programmes aimed at providing reproductive health services to all who need them. The Programme of Action acknowledges that domestic resources provide the largest portion of the funds needed, estimating that only about a third of those costs would come from external sources. The least developed countries and other low-income developing countries would require a greater share of external resources on a concessional and grant basis.

The Programme of Action encourages Governments to build partnerships with multilateral and donor agencies, civil society (including community-based organisations and non-governmental organisations) and the private sector, as appropriate, for the purpose of undertaking projects or developing programmes for the implementation of its recommendations. It also calls upon the international community to support South-South collaborative arrangements and facilitate direct South-South cooperation. At the programme level, it recommends national capacity-building for population and development and transfer of appropriate technology and know-how to developing countries. It also reiterates the call for the international community to "strive for the fulfilment of the agreed target of 0.7 per cent of gross national product for overall official development assistance and endeavour to increase the share of funding for population and development programmes commensurate with the scope and scale of activities required to achieve the objectives and goals" of the Programme of Action. The implementation of these recommendations would not only ensure the achievement of those goals and objectives but also contribute to building the global partnership for development called for in the United Nations Millennium Declaration.

10.5. Conclusion

Population is at the core of development, and population trends are a key element of the context in which development takes place. Consequently, measures directed towards influencing demographic behaviour and population dynamics, such as those contained in the Programme of Action of the International Conference on Population and Development and the key actions for its further implementation, would, if fully implemented, contribute significantly to the achievement of universally agreed development goals, including those in the United Nations Millennium Declaration. Implementation of the Programme of Action, particularly of measures to ensure that all couples and individuals have the number of children they desire and the information, education and means to do so, would contribute to accelerating the transition to low fertility in developing countries that still have high fertility levels, and would produce slower population growth, which in turn would improve the ability of those countries to adjust to future population increases, to combat poverty, to protect and repair the environment, and to set the conditions for sustainable development.

Even the difference of a single decade in the transition to stabilisation levels of fertility can have a considerable positive impact on quality of life. Furthermore, reduction of fertility gives rise to the "demographic bonus" whereby the proportion of the population of working age increases relative to that of children and the elderly, a change that can contribute significantly to economic growth and poverty reduction in contexts where governance facilitates human resource development and employment creation. Implementation of other recommendations included in the Programme of Action regarding the provision of education to all, especially girls and women, and increased investment in human resource development would also contribute to ensuring the benefits of the demographic bonus. Fulfilment of the goals and objectives of the Programme of Action would ensure the achievement of equivalent goals included in the United Nations Millennium Declaration, particularly reduction of child mortality and maternal mortality, universal access to primary education, parity in access to secondary and higher education between boys and girls, reductions in the spread of HIV, and achievement of gender equality and women's empowerment. Because of synergies between these goals and other universally agreed development goals, further benefits would be reaped. For instance, implementation of the Programme of Action would lead to both the empowerment of women in all spheres of life and a greater involvement of men in the exercise of reproductive rights and responsibilities. These achievements would contribute to enhancing economic growth and reducing poverty, reducing child mortality and improving maternal health, and reducing the spread of HIV. Similarly, improvements in education, particularly of girls, would contribute to reducing poverty, hunger, child and maternal mortality, and the spread of HIV, as well as promote gender equality. Furthermore, a better-educated population would likely change its demographic behaviour with respect to nuptiality, fertility, health and migration in ways leading to greater well-being.

Most developed countries exhibit fertility levels at or below the replacement level. Although most developing countries are far advanced in the transition from high to low fertility, some developing countries, mainly in Africa, still exhibit high fertility. Contraceptive use has increased significantly over the past decade, from 54 per cent in 1990 to 63 per cent in 2000. Short-acting and reversible methods are more popular in the developed countries, whereas longer-acting methods are more popular in the developing countries.

During the twentieth century, mortality experienced the most rapid decline in the history of humanity, owing to better hygiene, improved nutrition and medical practices based on scientific evidence. Until recently, it was expected that mortality would continue declining in all countries. However, HIV/AIDS has already produced marked increases in mortality in Africa, the region most affected by the disease. About 175 million persons reside in a country other than the one in which they were born. The number of migrants more than doubled between 1960 and 2000; 60 per cent of the world's migrants reside in the more developed regions. Affecting countries of origin, transit and destination, international migration is in the forefront of national and international agendas.

Developed and developing countries differ significantly with regard to their population concerns. High mortality, particularly infant and child mortality, maternal mortality and mortality related to HIV/AIDS, is the most significant population concern for developing countries. The most significant demographic concern of the developed countries relates to low fertility and its consequences, including population ageing and the shrinking of the working-age population. In sum, the current population picture is one of dynamic population change, reflected in new and diverse patterns of childbearing, mortality, migration, urbanisation and ageing. The continuation and consequences of these population trends present opportunities as well as challenges for all societies in the twenty-first century.

References

Bloom, D and Williamson, J., "Demographic transitions and economic miracles in emerging Asia", *World Bank Economic Review,* 1998.

Bloom, D.E, Canning, D and Sevilla, J., "The demographic dividend: a new perspective on the economic consequences of population change", *RAND Population Matters Monograph Series,* Santa Monica, California: RAND Corporation, 2003.

_______________ ., "Global demographic change: dimensions and economic significance, In Global demographic change: economic impacts and policy challenges", *proceedings of a symposium,* sponsored by the Federal Reserve Bank of Kansas City Jackson Hole, Wyoming - August 26-28, 2004.

Coale, A.J and Hoover, E.M., "Population growth and economic development in low-income countries", Princeton NJ: Princeton University Press, 1958.

Ehrlich, P., *The population bomb,* USA: Sierra Club Books, 1968.

Kuznets, S., "Population and economic growth", in *Proceedings of the American Philosophical Society,* III (3), 1967.

United Nations Population Division, *World population prospects,* the 2004 revision, United Nations, New York, February, 2005.

11

Demography and Social Development

11.1. Introduction

Economic growth in itself cannot be considered the be all and end all of development. By its very nature however, it may lead to improvement in social conditions, social justice, reduction of inequality, gender equity, and inclusion of all sections of society in the process of development. That is why the UNDP in 1990 started releasing the Human Development report to give comparative picture of different UN members countries on various aspects of human development. The appearance of shorter and shorter spans for reaching a certain level of economic prosperity in the countries during the second half of the 20th century gives the impression that more rapid economic development is feasible within a generation itself.

It is important to understand that every society has not one but a series of goals which it wants to achieve within a certain time span. Some of the goals within social development need not be fully supportive of each other and in fact, there could be some contradiction in the series of targets or goals, which the society may lay down for itself. However, revolutionary strides in technology and rapid development of the Information Communication Technologies (ICTs) has necessarily changed the perspectives of societies and the participants living there. Since information on what other societies have been able to achieve is now readily available by a click of a button, the goals or targets, which each society may like to give for itself have tended to converge.

It would be difficult to convince the public at large and the civil society to wait for 50 years now at the end of 2001. Similar hurry can be noticed in the demand for achievement of targets for replacement level of population, Health, for all, Rehabilitation facilities for the disabled, Empowerment of women, total elimination of child labour and Protection of all types of minorities.

While in the past centuries even the enlightened persons would have been willing to wait for a long time for achievement of such targets, this is no more so. The dangers of environmental degradation, the horrors of terrorism and those of the first and second world war including the nuclear holocausts, more or less make it imperative for national governments and policy makers to try to evolve a path of vary rapid social development.

One of the most serious problems of the 20th century was rapid population growth all over the world but even more so in already populous countries like India. The availability of various technologies to regulate human reproduction is rather recent and so is the situation about many other social components of development.

Fortunately, India has been aware of major developments in each of these areas and all the developments of the newer technologies for the service of humanity. It has also tried through its Five Year Plans, at least half-heartedly, to utilise all such technologies, methodologies and ways of organisations of human society during the last 50 years. But it has become clear for some time now that the existing modes of operation and utilisation of technologies are not good enough and would not be able to satisfy the urges of ordinary persons and of course, the enlightened sections of Indian society.

Therefore, it has become necessary to not only look at what was attempted during the process of planned development but also critically examine what was attempted during the process of planned development but also critically examine what was not achieved despite promises. This makes it even more important that targets of development of different components of social justice are not only revisited but also crosschecked with the reality of non-performance under various social heads.

11.2. Demographic Factors and its Impact

The data from the 2001 census, though not yet available in sufficiently desegregated forms can be considered both positive and negative for Indian social development - positive in the sense at that the rate of growth of population has certainly declined more or less in line with expectation generated by the earlier surveys about fertility and other basic demographic variables. The population figures for 2001 are certainly more than what would have been considered decent by the population policy makers or the national population commission. It was always difficult to believe that all the demographic goals set in the population policy would be achieved without major interventions from the government, the civil society or furies of nature or the three together.

Unlike many other countries, however, the Indian public is not unaware of the environmental degradation, which have already taken place and the difficulties of eking out a living in environmentally difficult tracts of the country. Since in quantitative and percentage terms the levels of migration in India from state to state are not very high for our larger size, the individual families are becoming more and more aware of difficulties generated due to shortages of various environmental resources and other factors which have also suddenly come up on the surface e.g., the awareness of likely HIV/AIDS disaster which has now been accepted as a strong possibility by the enlightened public and the civil society. Therefore, the 2001 census figures should be considered in balance, to be more on the positive side than on the negative and it can be expected that the demographic goals set out for the country as a whole and shown as achievable in a couple of states can be considered as feasible within the other states as well. In other words the demographic transition in the BIMARU States is not an impossibility in the medium to long term.

Trends in Fertility, Mortality, Nutrition and Health indicators have been studied in India for a long time. Indian demographers have been valued abroad for their expertise in the art and science of population projections. The same is true about Indian Population Census, which has shown remarkable continuity in the Census operation for almost a century. However, the processing of Census data, especially at the State and lower levels, takes a long time and adjustments to the census raw figure have to be made, in any case, for under-enumeration etc., like everywhere else. Therefore, the Government also undertakes sample surveys to understand family health and other characteristics.

These are the nature of sample registration system, RCH rapid household survey, ICMR surveys and of course, National Family Health Surveys, (two rounds already). Use of alternative assumptions for making projections of population does not make too much of difference to the total population of the older persons in the country as a whole but the situation would differ from state to state and on the basis of different assumptions. This is one category of people who need to be looked after by the society and if their proportion increases too fast, there would be excessive pressure on the working population to share their income with the very old and look after them in respect of health, disability, nutrition and other parameters of good living. On the other hand, if the fertility declines faster as per the assumption under NPP 2000, there would be decline in school going population with the consequent necessity of closing some primary/middle school and reduction in employment of teachers at the school stage as has already happened Kerala & Tamilnadu.

The 2001 Census results and other data from other surveys, mentioned earlier, throw light on the demographic behaviour of population in greater depth. The last NFHS survey indicated in details the demographically weak districts, mostly located in the BIMARU States plus Orissa, though there are some weak districts in other States as well. If the government intervention in this rather private behaviour pattern could be effective, as it is assumed to be so far, there is every reason for major government interventions in such demographically weak districts i.e. utilizing the base district unit for intervention rather than the state as a whole. With the break up of Bihar into two States, Jharkhand also has sufficiently large number of such weak districts to attend to along with J & K and the North-Eastern States.

The additional and new factors arising out of HIV/AIDS pandemic is also a matter of operational details to be worked out between the Central Government, on the one side and the other change agents, on the other. However, rising levels of literacy do not have that direct a correlation with reduction in HIV/AIDS as they have with levels of fertility. Therefore, much more efforts would be required to control the HIV/AIDS pandemic and rising rates of mortality associated with the same.

11.3. Employment Perspective

The distribution of employment over different economic activities is generally based on growth of different sectors of economy, which is never the same from year to year or from survey to survey. Thus, it is largely but wholly dependant on intra sectoral growth of different sectors. Alternatively or in contradictory terms, employment in national as well as international economies is affected by distribution of labour force by its age-sex-education-training levels. For example, if India did not have a reasonable surplus of educated and trained persons in the IT area, the IT component of the services sector would not have gone up rapidly, seen recently. It could not have also spared lakhs of personnel for employment abroad in the same field. Furthermore, if certain sectors of the economy are not perceived to be doing well the labour force likely to go to those sectors could possible change their educational/ skill composition or improve upon the previous base. The inter-play of growth in the various components of labour force is best demonstrated from the experience of urban females' entry into various types of employment in the new economy and thereby raise the labour force participation rate of the urban females as a whole. In this dynamic situation the past rate of unemployment of different sub-categories can at best be considered an approximation to the likely future behaviour of individual components of labour force, broken up by age, sex, residence, education/skill levels.

Since it is expected that much larger proportion of labour force would be residing in the Urban area by 2020 and since a large majority of them would have attained educational levels of primary and above, the dynamic behaviour of different components of labour force, mentioned above, would be even more difficult to project over the 20 years, in advance. Already the proportion of educated (matric and above) job seekers through the employment exchanges has gone well beyond 50% and could go even up to 80%, if the experience of metropolitan cities like

Delhi can be considered pointer to the future. The recent decline in the observed rate of labour force between 1993-94 and 1999-2000 to as low as 1.03% p.a. may not be terribly accurate but is definitely a pointer to a clear decline in the growth rate. It appears that the Planning Commission is not very sure of this low growth rate and is likely to utilise growth rate of 1.8% p.a. for the purposes of projections of labour force in the Tenth Plan. At this stage, there are no known definite reasons for such a major drop in the growth of labour force in the recent five year survey period and till these factors are fully analysed and understood, it could only be said that increase in the number of years spent in the educational institutions is a very likely causative factor. Considering that India still has a very low average number of years of education per capita as per the latest HDR, the effect of higher and greater use of educational/skill opportunities is likely to remain with us all through the period up to 2020.

The growth of labour force in the age group 15-29 has to be watched very carefully since the members of this age group display and have displayed in the past rather high rate of unemployment. There is a hypothesis with international experts that unemployment rate continue to grow from the level of illiterates to the level of education below university and it decline thereafter i.e. there is an inverted U curve to display the pattern of unemployment rate. There is a parallel with the labour force participation for the same educational levels but this is better represented by the U curve. Recent evidence of unemployment of the educated above secondary level i.e. degree holder, technical diploma holders and above is quite disconcerting. The technical diploma holders and above are displaying almost the highest rates of unemployment, which are potentially unsustainable.

There could be various factors to explain this strange behaviour but no collection of cost and other expenditure from the beneficiaries of such education from public institutions could certainly be one of them. The other factor of relatively low quality of degree level/technical personnel from most of the institutions is also at work but both the parents and students suffer from what is called 'diploma disease', otherwise explained as paper qualification syndrome. The holders of paper qualifications compete for a limited number of jobs in the market organized labour since the Government sector is already showing a decline, this leads to competition for displaying a bigger/higher ability by individual job seeker to the potential employers. There are already a large number of personnel with degree/diploma and the employers are utilising the certificate basically as a screening mechanism. Therefore, if everyone in the labour market raises his educational profile one notch, the employers remain as uninformed of the potential ability of the candidates as before. The only solution to this syndrome would be to raise the private cost of higher education to the beneficiaries so that every one does not want to accumulate more certificates as a tool of competition for limited jobs in the formal labour market. Most countries, including some developing countries, are moving in that direction and there is no reason to doubt that India will also move in the same direction though with a time lag.

Another factor in a liberalised and pre-dominantly service economy is the share of female employment in the total work force. With continuous decline of employment in agricultural/farming, there is evidence of increase in non-farm sector even in the rural areas/labour force. This tendency of the non-farm sector to grow has been studied for some time and there is no doubt that like in other countries, non-farm sector both in terms of output and employment is growing in our rural areas. An important issue therefore, is quality of work likely to be available in rural areas when the increased availability of education and skills is going to raise the expectations of individual females for better quality work not merely tending of animals, forestry and other traditional occupations other than agricultural. If the economy continues to grow at 6-7-8 % p.a. it is likely that the diversification of rural economy would generate a lot of employment opportunities, especially in the Service sectors.

Since creation of social infrastructure is an accepted goal, both for urban and rural areas, females, especially educated females are likely to get the benefit of the maintenance of social infrastructure, be it health, education or social work, care of aged and disabled and so on. Therefore, there are reasons to believe that the gap between the rate of participation of labour force between sexes would decline overall and more so in the younger age group. The males on the other hand, would have to compete with educated females especially in the service sector and within the subsector of 'Community, Social and personal' services. This is also because females are likely to accept part-time jobs while males prefer and need full time jobs of a more regular type to be able to support dependents on a sustained basis.

The worldwide experience however, points to significant reduction in manual jobs, a typical preserve of males. The trends are also pointing against any further increase in blue-collar jobs of manufacture/ transport & related sectors. The livelihood is therefore that of more and more under-employment for the male who would complain and demand a better job whereas the female might not do so aggressively. Many of these hypotheses are based on experiences of economic growth of difference types of economies/countries. Since India is practically open to all new technologies and has voted for ICT's, the direction of growth in India cannot be very different from the emerging market economies like Korea, Malaysia and the industrialised parts of Greater China.

Another macro factor to be taken into consideration is whether the recent reversal of growth of labour force below that of the population would continue all through to 2020 or would it revert to the previous pattern of the labour force growing faster than population. Based on the latest available growth rate of 1.03%, it would be difficult to assume that in the future also there would be much lower growth rate of labour force than population. In fact, the two growth rates might converge closer by the year 2020, as has happened in many developed countries. The other macro factors relate to need for 'Decent work' on the one hand and remunerative work for older people, on the other.

The ILO has recently examined the issue of quality of work at the international level and has recommended to all ILO members the need to emphasise on better quality work than available so far to the masses. India is expected to fall in line with this emphasis and try its best to provide better quality work to the majority of population over the next 20 years. This would obviously imply better occupational safety and health and less accidents all the work places. This would naturally include the major occupation of agriculture and related activities where the current Indian work force does not seem to be bothered.

11.3.1. Child Labour

Since by its very nature, child labour cannot be decent work. The ILO studies in many places have indicated that replacement of child labour by the adult labour could possibly increase the final cost of product by about 2% but up to a maximum of 5%. Given the fact that the cost of labour as a proportion of total cost of a physical product has continuously fallen while the share of other intermediaries has arisen, on pure economic grounds there is not much justification for continuance of child labour. Over and above the lack of economic rationale expect for isolated groups of families in special circumstances, there is also the need for providing the basic factors of growth of the child, both physical nutrition and intellectual stimulus.

The country has already passed a law for making elementary education a Fundamental Right for all children in the age group 6-14 years, as already laid down in the Indian Constitution. As the law starts getting implemented, more and more children would be withdrawn systematically from the labour force and brought into school education. In terms of employment planning, such total elimination would not change the total volume of labour force since by definition the labour force has already eliminated child labour in official calculation. However, once a child reaches Grade 8 or so, the curiosity generated by the educational programmes could possibly push him to go to higher grades and to that extent also reduce the participation rate in the labour force in the higher age group 15-29 years.

11.3.2. Older Persons

The question of older persons' participation in work is far more complicated since the life expectancy now is around 64 years and the number of persons above 60 years has already reached 75 millions. It has to be analysed whether all of them are resting or a large proportion is engaged in economic activities. The worldwide projection of persons above 60 years is around 600 millions which could rise to 1100 million by 2025. In India the proportion of older persons i.e. above 65 years is shown to be between 6.4 and 6.7%.

In many countries people continue to work till the age 65 and in the Indian rural areas and even in the urban informal sector, there is no retirement age as such. Therefore, a significant proportion of persons above 60 years is already working and, over the next 20 years, this is likely to rise further, implying the need for focusing all the efforts more on the older group of 65+, rather than 60+. The current estimates made by several knowledgeable persons/organisations indicate that the situation of even the 60+ is rather hopeless, with 40% living below the poverty line, 73% illiterate and 12 million i.e. 16% are blind for want of cataract operation. Over and above the bland figures, is the change in the social system with extended family breaking up into nuclear families. However, the positive picture lies in the fact that almost 80% of the current 60+ are in rural area where the extended family is breaking up more slowly. The problem could however, become acute over the next 20 years even in rural areas if current trends persist and no major interventions take place.

By the year 2020, even if we take the lower figure of 6.4% as the proportion of 65+, the total number is going to be rather significant i.e. over 80 million as against the current year estimate of 75 million of 60+. With continuous degradation of environment and shortages of clean air and water and other environmental resources, it is obvious that this group of over 80 million persons would need special attention, both from the Government and the Civil society/younger members of the family. Given the fact that there are no private retirement pension plans and the existing efforts to start them are developing rather slowly, major interventions from the society are required for the benefit of 65+ by 2020.

Some of the recommendations made above are based on experience of Western countries where old age home is the accepted model of delivery of Government-funded health care and other facilities. The cost calculations made by other experts however, indicate that the western style of old age home is beyond the means of Indian economy even by the year 2020 and that the community-based approach is likely to be the cost effective alternative. Even in some developed countries like Japan, the older persons are linked up with very young children, which is likely to be more satisfactory than plain dependence on the income earning of the young people through the mechanism of old age homes etc.

11.3.3. Gender Equity

Another issue relating to employment as well as Human development is that of gender equity. It is well known that women suffer from discrimination in the work place whether in the organised or the unorganised sector. It is also well known that within the various occupations and economic activities available, women tend to concentrate on the traditional occupations or those, which require less/new technologies and less manual work. The rates of participation of women in the labour force are already much lower in practically all age groups, especially if we focus on main workers. However, in terms of marginal workers women out-number men significantly but even more than this is the fact that a lot of work done by women is invisible to the accountants of GDP. While many efforts have been made to bring on the surface different types of work, which is of economic nature even in the household, the overall GDP figures still do not reflect the true contribution of women to the output of goods and services. However, this is so not only for India but also in most countries, even more in the developing world. At one time, some studies were organized to identify what was called women-prone occupations, which showed that in a large number of manual occupations women constituted the dominant proportion, especially coal mining and construction work. Therefore, the picture of developed world about women- related occupations is not true of India now and might not be true even by the year 2020. Unless there is major shift of work force from out of farming/ agriculture to non-farm occupations the continuing discrimination against women in the work place is detrimental to their health needs, apart from educational and personal care needs. It is difficult to visualise to what extent the quality of life for an average woman, leaving aside the matric and higher educated, would improve by the year 2020. It is however, very clear that without massive doses of education and skills and improvement in their ability to control reproduction, these improvements would be only minor.

It is already known that intra-family nutrition distribution is against women and children or women and girl children, as against males. The earning male member obviously and naturally, gets higher food intake and better care and so also the male child.

This discrimination can perhaps be removed without much economic cost in view of the fact that total nutrition availability in the country has surely improved. It is expected that by 2020 the nutritional availability would further improve and therefore, without much economic costs the intra-family distribution of nutrition should also improve. Logically this should lead to lower proportion of low birth babies, lower birth related problems for women, less anaemia and possibly better ability to master new skills, so far kept by the males for themselves.

Better regulation of environmental factors and higher availability of better fuel in the rural/poor family, should also lead to less pollution related difficulties for the women working in the kitchens. Better fuel availability should in fact, also reduce the number of hours spent on fuel collection & combustion and therefore, leave more time personal care/health care. Further, availability of birth attendants for every single birth, registration of births and deaths and child care through the ICDS route should also, help in reducing the drudgery and quantity of physical work for women and thereby allow them to participate in better quality work within and outside the household. While considering the questions of gender equity, one cannot forget the stark differences, which have already come up between states.

The gender development index prepared by the UNDP places India at the 108th rank amongst 174 countries. However, using the same methodology if similar indexes are prepared for different states, one finds Kerala to be similar to medium-development countries while the BIMARU states are similar to LDCs in the UN ranking. This means that no simple strategy of development will work for all the states together.

The process of awareness generation and education are essential for any efforts towards gender equality. This would for example, include campaign to reverse the low sex ratio in most of the country which is based on gender discrimination at birth or even before birth. Integration of health services in a more coordinated manner would also help in this process towards reduction of anaemia, better nutrition and provision of good health care and feeding practices. In fact, one of the factors working against good nutritional status is the fact of poor food preparation practices, which lose a lot of nutrition in the very process of food preparation. Literacy for women is a very important component of all these efforts and happily, there is a good chance that very soon there would be no district with less than 50 % female literacy, which appears to be a very important mile stone.

11.3.4. Vulnerable Groups

Every democratic society has to cope up with the care of those who cannot care for themselves un-aided. These include a whole range of people for example, the handicapped persons either due to visual or hearing or speech or orthopaedic problems and those who are mentally challenged. Another way of looking at the vulnerable sections of society is to examine the whole group of Scheduled Castes, STs, socially and educationally backward classes and minorities. The last group is that of the crime prone persons or sections of society including groups of families in some parts of the country.

While some data is available on the SC and ST groups of population as a result of considerable work over the last century, not much data is available on the persons handicapped due to other factors. Similarly, not much data on the motivation of the crime prone individuals, family or groups is readily available. This shortage of data or poor quality data makes it difficult to develop depend able projections up to 2020. But the Government of India already has a number of institutions and departments whose job it is to analyse the situation of each such group or section of individuals.

The Ministry of Social Justice along with the Rehabilitation Council of India and several other organisations is the most important single ministry to assist in the process of main-streaming the disabled of various kinds, into normal life and participate in all types of activities of a normal society. Over the 1990s the Government of India have enacted new laws and strengthened the legislative framework for assistance to persons with disability, along with specific rehabilitation mechanisms. It is too early to say whether these mechanisms and law/regulation are sufficient for the purpose of mainstreaming persons with disability into normal life. But it is already well known that only a few buildings and some transport/ public facilities are actually accessible to the disabled persons. It is obvious that creation of non-handicapping physical environment is an absolutely basic requirement for assisting such persons. Even more, the central initiatives do not get translated well into the state governments' actions and even less at the operational level of districts. For example, rehabilitation services as per the relevant Act should have been able to reach each district through 'district rehabilitation centre' which must work as a single window facilitation centre for all requirement of persons with disabilities.

Though 'integrated education' has been the favourite theme at the school level for a couple of decades, the actual number of students who are able to take advantage of integrated education is much less. There are cultural factors at work against persons with obvious disabilities in a tradition-ridden society like India, which might explain the relatively lower number of persons, picked up in the NSS survey in 1991. Even worse, many parents would not like to admit that their wards are disabled. There are now newer afflictions at work also, including HIV/AIDS, drug abuse and road accidents, which are likely to increase continuously. Finally, mental illness is hardly diagnosed in a traditional society whether rural and urban, and mental disorders tend to be ignored even by the educated persons for a long time.

From this angle it is clear that India has a very long way to go since we have serious problems due to various diseases, lack of sanitation, poor drinking water, poor care of expectant mothers including poor nutrition and bias against those born with a disability and against the girl children. As regards attention to persons already suffering

from disability including self-made disability arising out of drug abuse, the institutional care available is very minor and does not really reach the remote parts of even normal districts. Over and above the cultural factors and in-appropriate traditions, there is a problem of finding sufficient funds for looking after the disabled persons, despite a variety of organizations and ministries/departments in various governments.

The system of special school, clinic, home based learning, institutional care for the drug dependents, and so on, is obviously too costly for a country with our per capita income and therefore, alternative modes of delivery of care have to be developed through the community NGOs and even Gram Panchayats but under the overall scientific and technical guidance of the state level apparatus.

11.3.5. Other Groups

As for the groups of SC, ST and OBCs , considerable work has been done by various government organisations and various Commissions have been set up under the Constitution to supervise all such government funded actions. However, it has to be admitted that most of the benefits of development out of government funds have not spread widely across the entire spectrum of SCs or STs and of course, OBCs. It has also been recognised by now, right up to the level of Supreme Court that a lot of benefit of reservation of jobs and facilities or school places has been appropriated by the creamy layers of such groups.

The development of SCs, STs and OBCs has therefore, to be seen in this larger context of a huge variety of situations under which individual castes or tribes might be labouring. However, it is difficult to work out separate caste or tribe-specific operational strategies since this could be struck down in the Courts. A number of studies have been made on what type of castes or tribes have been left out from availing the major benefits flowing from central Government funds and it is possible that some non-justiciable interventions could be made in their favour, in comparison to other castes/ tribes also covered under the heading SC-ST.

As regards the OBCs, the experience available is not good enough to demand any major change of government approach to their development but it must be noticed that the demands to be categorised an as OBC in the hope of government employment is now self defeating in a liberal or liberalizing Indian economy. This is because most of the wealth formation is now expected to take place outside the Government and in fact, at the national level the number of government jobs is now on a declining trend. Even if some of states are not yet on this trend, they are most likely to be so by 2020 and therefore, such states have also to find other means of assisting the individual SCs, STs and OBCs.

11.3.6. Minorities

The government also has the responsibility of assistance to the minorities including Muslims Christians, Sikhs, Buddhists and Zoroastrians. They together account for 17 or more percent of national population and there are 142 districts in the country, which have in their population more than 20% minorities. The current government thinking is to assist the minorities through education including technical education, special attention to their health and housing needs and priority sector lending in their favour etc. especially to artisan and handloom weaver etc. where the minorities have concentration in many parts of the country.

11.3.7. Social Defence

Though India is not a high crime society and respect for law in the general public is still high, there is a rising trend in various type of crimes, practically all over the country. However, the reported crime numbers or crime rates always remain much lower than the reality and over and above this is the failure of the criminal justice system to track down crimes firstly and then to give them proper punishment in good time so as to act as a deterrent to other criminals. It is feared that with the spread/availability of ICTs and rapid economic growth, organised crime could acquire a more volitional and disruptive form, along side emergence of terrorism, environment crimes and now cyber crimes. It is also feared that rapid economic growth in many parts of the country could create imbalances and disparities between the rich and the poor.

The growth of slum and unauthorised colonies in practically all the cities and un-regulated urbanisation itself tends to encourage a smart persons with criminal tendencies to develop crime in an organised way, be it drug trafficking, prostitution or trafficking in women and children. Therefore, the potential of growth of crime and criminals in India by the 2020 is truly high. Given the fact that India is considered to be a poorly governed or at least a soft state, organisation of crime or crime syndicates appears to be easier than before.

The existence of stark poverty in many groups of society, the patent discrimination against SCs and STs and other lower castes is itself a factor for growth of crime. The feeling of discrimination is further aggravated by ability of the relatively rich to avoid taxes and commit other economic offences without commensurate punishment. The economic and social marginal of poor also adds to the growth of diseffective children, adolescence and young adults who are frustrated with their lot. There are however, a number of new laws to protect against the atrocious on the vulnerable sections of society and children and happily, the upper judiciary is proactive in enforcing the provision of such laws and regulations.

In the back drop of a rapidly changing crime situation experts feels that a correlation strategy, widespread reform in the prison system and that of Juvenile justice are not only required urgently but could be even useful in improving modification for good economic growth. However, it is also realise that the system incarceration of individual, young or adult, is to costly for a country with low per capita income. Therefore, non-custodial measures have been recommended for the significant component of offenders facing criminal justice system and courts. It is also noticed that public participation in prevention of crime as well as in treatment and rehabilitation of offender is highly desirable. In the light of low per capita income, this is perhaps more effective than the Western style major for increasing and reforms of the prison system and similar other facilities. The United Nations has given a lot of thought and made recommendation toward utilising the non-custodial system for the purpose where the civil society, relevant NGOs, community policing and voluntary efforts would play a much higher role than before. It is however, distrait to note that very few organisation are active in the work of main-streaming of social deviants/criminal.

11.4. Conclusion

The examination of various social dimensions in the light of expected rapid growth of the economy must be seen the large context of a relatively secure society and peace at the national border. India with its vast land and maritime borders, is already committed to additional resource for national defence. This is become urgent in the light of terrorist attacks of 11 September which has bought turbulence and instability closed to our hilly borders and perhaps, to the entire country.

References

Johnston, Denis F. and Michael J. Carley, "Social Measurement and Social Indicators", *Annals of the American Academy of Political and Social Science*, 1981.

Kutta, Fratisek, Michal Illner, "System of Social Indicators and Elaboration of the Information Basis for Social Planning and Forecasting", *Sociologicky-Casopis*, 1983.

Land, Kenneth C., "Social Indicators", *Annual Review of Sociology*, Vol. 9: 1-26, 1983.

Mangahas, Mahar, "Measurement of Poverty and Equity: Some ASEAN Social Indicators Experience", *Social Indicators Research*, 1983.

12

Population and Employment Issues

A significant change in inequality in income and wealth is possible only in a longer-term perspective. Employment structure of an economy is the normal instrument that can cause a change in inequality either way, i.e. an increase or a decrease in the inequality. Other economic instruments such as target group policies and programmes have a short-term impact, but the redistribution through employment is sustainable. Since the governments function within the administrative and fiscal constraints, the target group programmes normally have a marginal impact on income redistribution. Income of labour enables flow of resources across income classes of people and across the social and ethnic groups. Flows of income across locations are influenced both by assets available and by other modes of creating employment opportunities. However, income generated by employment of migrant labour, facilitates flow of resources across regions for a given regional distribution of capital assets. Employment and equity of income across classes of people and across regions are, therefore, closely related to each other in the long term.

12.1. Age Structure of Population

The size of economically active population is determined by the age structure. Population growth will reduce from the current level of 1.95 per cent per annum to about 1.25 per cent by 2020. Growth of population in the working age group (15 to 59) is at present around 2.4 per cent, substantially higher than growth of overall population. This will continue to be so for many years. Convergence between growth of population and that in the age group 15-59 years occurs around the year 2030. Since labour force participation is not uniform across age groups, the size of labour force is influenced by age structure. Participation in labour force i.e. the labour force participation rate (LFPR) is influenced by need to work versus other alternative uses of one's time. A unidirectional relationship between growth of population and labour force has not been observed in the past.

Some decline in labour force growth could be due to a lower growth in population, which also implies a slower growth in working age population. However, the decline in labour force growth from 2.29% per annum to 1.03% between 1983/1993-94 and 1993-94/1999-2000 is too sharp to be explained by deceleration in population growth alone. Deceleration in population growth during this period has to be seen together with the decline in Labour Force Participation Rates (LFPRs) for a possible explanation.

12.1.1. Labour Force Participation

The decline in participation rates observed during 1993-94 to 1999-2000 needs to be carefully examined in terms of trends in different segments of the population and by different age groups and in a longer-term perspective. The decline in the LFPR in the younger age group reflects longer term trend of shift in activity status of this group towards education. This trend is likely to continue in future. Similarly, in the age group 60 and above the decline in the LFPR can be explained by increase in the share of more aged in the 60 and above population, where the LFPRs are expected to be low. In a few cases the declines are sharper and the reasons need to be looked into. In this background, the future projections of labour force in relation to working age population have to be considered. The participation rates for younger age groups have dropped much more than other age groups. In the 10-14 years age group, the decline will be to near zero in the next 5 to 8 years as elementary education becomes compulsory.

12.1.2. Labour Force Skills

Income of labour i.e. its wage level is determined by productivity. Both the technology used (i.e. capital intensity) and the skill level of worker determines labour productivity. It is not easy to quantify the level of skills in the labour force because data on skill levels are not readily available. It is evident that education levels in the labour force in India are very low. About 44.0 % of all workers in 1999-2000 were illiterate and another 22.7% had schooling only up to the primary level. A positive feature of the situation is that education levels will improve over time because the younger age groups are much better educated.

The system is excessively oriented towards general academic education with little or no vocational orientation. The preference for general education is driven primarily by the perception that an academic degree is necessary to obtain a government job, which is highly valued because job security is virtually complete and pay scales are typically much above market wages. The net result is that the education system has neglected the need to provide vocational skills and to generate awareness and demand among students for acquiring, marketable skills.

12.2. Demand for Labour

The preparation of a longer-term vision for employment must take into consideration the developments taking place on the supply side of labour while planning for a strategy to absorb the annual additions to the labour force. The longer-term vision, however, needs to look beyond mere absorption of the labour force in any activity irrespective of the quality of work that an activity can offer in terms of improving the living conditions of workers. Ten Million Employment Opportunities per year has established that with slightly altering the structure of growth in favour of labour intensive sectors , it is possible to achieve the overall balancing between the supply of labour and demand for labour, even in a shorter term perspective. Also, the demand for labour thus generated will be of gainful nature in terms of ensuring availability of work on a regular basis. However, the larger question of improving the income and productivity levels of existing workers and those who are likely to enter the labour force within the perspective period can be squarely addressed only in a longer term perspective. This would call for concerted efforts on many fronts, some of which are discussed below.

12.2.1. Structure of Economy

Input of labour in production process depends upon technology used, and technology used varies across the industries. Traditional agriculture is more labour intensive than the modern manufacturing industries. With the modernisation of economy, share of agriculture in workforce reduces due to two factors; food demand grows at a much slower pace at high levels of income, which moderates the demand for food-grains. Secondly, the technology used in agriculture, at higher yield levels is much less labour absorbing than traditional agriculture.

The secular decline in the importance of agriculture sector in the overall economic structure is a part of economic development. Work Opportunities that are lost in traditional agriculture have to be replaced by work opportunities in some other sector. In the normal course it is the secondary sectors (manufacturing, electricity and construction) that grow much faster than agriculture during transition of an economy. However, in the post reform period the growth of manufacturing industries has been constrained by competition from imports. Thus, in the medium term, the ability of manufacturing sector to replace the work opportunities lost in traditional agriculture is rather limited over the next 5 to 10 years. However, there are immense possibilities for diversification in agricultural sector towards more value added activities such as food processing. This is an area, which has by and large remained unexploited, because reforms in agriculture sector having been very slow, resources have not yet started flowing into food processing industries. Involvement of State Governments in implementing reforms in agriculture and food processing sectors is of crucial importance. Economic returns from States initiatives in transforming the rural economy from traditional agriculture to more value added activities in horticulture, etc. has been demonstrated well in some of the States, such as Maharashtra and Himachal Pradesh. Such diversification has immense potential for bridging some of the gaps in productivity levels of workers in agriculture vis a vis other sectors.

Besides diversification of agriculture there is a strong need to restructure the rural economy by way of promotion of non farm activities in rural areas. Whatever non-farm activities are being carried out in the rural areas now are more out of a desperation to eke out a living rather than an informed choice of a vocation, backed by infrastructural and institutional facilities. A massive improvement in infrastructure is required to promote growth of rural industries on a sustainable basis. This will go a long way in generating good quality employment and meeting many of the consumption requirements of rural people. Many steps have been taken in regard to village connectivity, e.g., Prime Minister Gram Sarak Yojana (PMGSY) and telecommunication. But power sector reforms are urgently needed to set up modern processing facilities. Another area requiring attention is tackling the bottlenecks in the availability of business services institutions - training, banking, insurance, storage facilities etc.

12.2.2. Formal and Informal Sector

In the current phase of economic reforms, a sharp deceleration in growth of organised sector has been observed. This has largely occurred because employment opportunities in public sector and Government have stagnated since 1994.

One definition of organised sector is based on its capital intensity, i.e., the technology used. Other definition of organised sector is in terms of employment - the terms of contract between the employer and employee. At present the terms of employment are seen to be rigid by the organised sector, with the result that though organised sector needs and uses a lot of labour input, it does not show up in jobs created. Similar tendencies have forced the capital intensity to increase even in the small-scale sector. One of the suggestions has been that, if employment is the social purpose of a small-scale policy or small and medium enterprise policy then the policy should be designed in terms of jobs created rather than investments made. The growth of formal sector (i.e., organised sector) has to be based on private sector in future.

There are two factors, which would severely affect the prospects of organised sector of employment, as it is presently defined, emerging as a major employer even in a 20 years perspective. Firstly, the base of the sector is very small and therefore the overall impact of even a very fast growth of employment in these sectors will be only marginal. Secondly, within the organised sector, the employment growth potential in the Public sector, which accounts for approximately 70% of the total organised employment, is very limited. The above two factors coupled with the declining employment elasticity in the sector preclude emergence of this sector as a major job provider in the near future.

In this scenario, the predominance of informal sector, including agriculture, is likely to continue and therefore the concerns of the smaller establishments (informal sector), which are crucial to its growth, and also of the workers, which is today a vulnerable lot, need to be attended to. Marginal improvement in the tools used by the artisans, access to institutional credit, some amount of skill orientation and the general information about the availability of markets for different products will improve the performance of the sector as well as help the individual workers immensely.

The reach of the social security benefits are largely restricted to the workers in the formal or the organised sector barring a few attempts to reach the informal sector workers through welfare boards. A large proportion of the workers are still left out of any system of social security. There is a need to earnestly address to the welfare needs of the workers in the informal sector. This does not necessarily require bringing the sector under the purview of labour laws. Introduction of labour laws might kill the greatest advantage that this sector has in terms of flexibility in operation, through rigidities, which are generally inherent in application of such laws. This also cannot be done on the basis of an employer-employee relationship, as in the organised sector, because majority of the workers in informal sector are self-employed. Only through a participatory approach between the governments and the workers can emerge a sustainable system of social security for informal sector workers.

12.2.3. Labour Laws

The existing labour laws framework does not encourage growth of labour intensive sectors as matter of design. These laws need to be reviewed in such a manner that it introduces an element of incentive for greater labour absorption. A holisitic review of the labour laws is under consideration at various foras. The guiding principle of any such review has to be encouraging faster absorption of labour, without sacrificing the core welfare concerns of labour.

12.3. Patterns of Labour Migration

Depending upon the stage of demographic transition a State has achieved and also on the likely growth pattern, the experience of different States in terms of labour force growth and employment generation is likely to be varied. This would have implications for the inter State variations in the incidence of unemployment and also on the migration of labour in search of work.

A typology of states based on growth of labour force and changes in employment rate shows that in States of Andhra Pradesh, Gujarat, Haryana, Karnataka, Maharashtra, Tamil Nadu and West Bengal, the labour force growth will be falling and unemployment rate will also fall, given the employment - GDP elasticity in these States. However, in the States of Bihar, Rajasthan, and Uttar Pradesh, not only the unemployment rate will be rising but growth of labour force will also be accelerating. These patterns suggest the States of origin and destination States of migrant labour.

Migration will increase in the long terms, as the work opportunities in traditional agriculture shrink. Normally, the migrants are at the receiving end in the destination States because they have little political voice. However, better skilled migrants have better income levels and can thereby adjust better. Migrants' jobs are hardly ever-single employer ones. They frequently change the employers and alternate between the wage employed and self-employed status. In this long-term perspective, a social security system for unorganised workers that is designed for such transient employment categories will have to be developed.

12.3.1. Private Investment

The web of controls created by the government over the decades is a virtual jungle whose profile is well known, but whose details are not known so well known. It covers every sector of the economy but remains particularly oppressive in areas where government was an active producer/supplier, such as physical infrastructure (railways, power, irrigation & drainage, urban utilities), social sectors (education, health) and mining. It also remains in factor markets.

The broad approach to market reform is familiar. That is to promote competition wherever it is possible to do so and to mimic competition (introduce benchmark competition) through enlightened professional regulation where there are natural monopoly elements. Thus for instance, the first step in railway reform could be to allow the private sector to provide train services (while keeping the rail network under the Indian Railways). There is still not sufficient understanding, however, of the difference between professional regulation for development of the industry in the long-term interests of consumers and interventionist controls to force extraneous consideration and interests upon it. Thus identifying and eliminating the latter and defining and implementing the former requires detailed study of each sector/sub-sector, hard work and determination to overcome self seeking arguments and vested interests.

12.3.2. Railway Policy Reform

Private competition has recently been allowed in the area of movement of containers over the railway network. Private participation is being considered for building/operating the high-speed freight corridors.

12.3.2.1. Regulator

The RRA would have authority over pricing of 'natural monopoly' elements and over the conditions & quality of supply. It must also promote competition wherever possible and forbear price control in potentially competitive segments. The RRA must ensure nondiscriminatory access by new rail service companies to the 'natural monopoly' rail track network i.e. on the same terms and conditions as those available to the Owner Company. The railway tracks along with signalling equipment constitutes a 'natural monopoly.' Pricing of the 'natural monopoly' networks and ensuring fair access to this network by new competitors is the most difficult job for the regulator. This job is facilitated if the natural monopoly network or segment is separated from the service provision functions.

12.3.2.2. Investment De-licensing

Complete investment de-licensing is necessary to ensure that the public users get the full benefits of competition. Global experience is that the monopoly provider, who has the incentive & the means, works to undermine competition. The regulator with the support of the users must actively thwart the monopolist in the interests of the public. Investment must be fully de-licensed, with no artificial barriers.

12.3.3. Agriculture Employment

Indian agriculture's share of value added has declined in line with the fall in demand for cereals and food that we would expect with rising per capita incomes. The "double dualism" has however had the effect of slowing the shift of labour out of agriculture. This can be seen from a cross-country comparison of the share of agriculture in Value Added and employment. India's share of agricultural value added is marginally higher than the trend line, but agriculture's share of total employment is way above what we would expect at its level of per capita GDP.

12.3.4. Modern Services

Contrary to a perception that the share of Value added from Manufacturing is too low and that from Services is too high in total value added both are marginally higher than the cross-country trend line. Among the high growth economies India has had the third highest increase in the share of services in value added (13.7%) since 1980 after Hong Kong and Luxembourg. Somewhat surprisingly China had the fourth highest increase of 11.6% points.

12.3.5. Manufacturing Services

The first noteworthy fact is that the average rate of growth of services has been faster than that for manufacturing in every sub-phase i.e. since mid-sixties. Despite this the share of services is in line with our per capita GDP. Second, modern services have grown faster than modern manufacturing and traditional services have grown faster than traditional manufacturing since sub-phase IB. As a consequence the share of traditional manufacturing and services has remained more or less constant during the reform phase.

Though the relatively fast growth of modern services can be sustained till India reaches the high income category this will not necessarily result in a faster shift of the labour force out of agriculture. By definition modern services are more capital intensive (K/L) and less labour using than traditional services.

Their degree of capital intensity varies just as it does within the modern manufacturing sector. It is likely, however, that on average modern services are more educated/skilled labour intensity (H/L) than modern manufacturing. Thus faster growth of modern services implies faster growth of demand for educated/skilled labour than for unskilled labour. Therefore unless the policy distortions that constrain modern labour intensive manufacturing are addressed the problem of excess labour in agriculture and the rural-urban poverty gap would be difficult to solve.

12.3.6. Manufacturing Productivity

Historically the most important driver of productivity change in low and lower middle-income countries have been the shift of labour from agriculture to modern industry. In India the proportion of the total labour force in manufacturing has increased marginally from 10.2% in 1977-8 to 11% 1999-2000 while the share of GDP from manufacturing has risen from 13.6% of total GDP to 16.7% of total over the same period. The structural shift of labour continues to be stymied in India by inflexible labour laws that discourage hiring of (unskilled) labour in organised industry (and services) and encourage the adoption of (unskilled) labour saving technology. The adoption of capital intensive technology in modern manufacturing results in faster capital deepening and lower aggregate TFP growth than would have prevailed under flexible labour laws, though productivity continues to increase. This contrasts with the performance of S. E Asian countries with more flexible labour laws, which have simultaneously had higher rates of growth in manufacturing employment and Value added and in overall growth than India.

12.3.6.1. Labour flexibility

The key to re-balancing India's employment structure and sustaining higher TFPG levels is increased labour flexibility, the modern democratic equivalent of competition in the labour market. Modern social democratic societies apply a different metric to competition in labour markets (involving flesh and blood human beings) than they do to markets for goods and services. Only in a dictatorship or communist country can "hire and fire" really mean what the Indian left accuses it of being in democratic countries.

Germany and France have among the most rigid labour laws in Europe, while continental Europe is recognised to have more rigid laws than the USA and UK. In Germany workers would feel that it is their responsibility and right to work hard and produce quality output. It would be unthinkable for workers to believe or expect that they will not be fired if they shirk work. Even in France where they may object to a profitable company firing its workers and moving its operations to another country, no one would question the right of a company to reduce its work force when demand falls sharply. If we can change our mindset and make essential changes in the laws, rules and procedures, the structural transformation of the economy could resume with consequent acceleration in TFPG.

Companies providing contract labour should be responsible for abiding by and meeting the obligations of labour law and not the companies using the labour. The latter should be free to use contract labour for any purpose for which the former are willing to provide contract labour. There should be no restrictions on the setting up of companies to provide contract labour. Part of this could perhaps be done by identifying and changing some of the rules.

12.3.7. Competition in Education

One of the important failings of Indian socialism was the gross neglect of literacy and primary education. The contrast is particularly glaring when we compare with communist-socialist countries such as the USSR, Eastern Europe and Maoist China, who achieved a high level of education for the general population/labour force. One of the less noticed consequences of this neglect is the poor (average) quality of services and goods of common consumption generally produced by the small-scale sector and Khadi & Village industries.

With reforms the rate of growth of the sector could be doubled and its quality improved manifold without an excessive strain on limited government revenues. The education sector in India can be transformed within a span of 3 to 5 years given the right mix of policy, regulation and reorientation of government expenditure. This in turn can have a profound impact on the quality of output in all sectors of the economy and the competitiveness of Indian industry, services and agriculture.

12.3.8. Electricity

The third policy reform that is capable of structurally transforming the Indian economy is electricity reform. Some of our analysis suggests that electricity supply by government monopolies has been the most important (infrastructure) constraint on overall economic growth. It is the only component of infrastructure that turns out to be statistically significant in growth regressions and FDI analysis. A condition of excess supply of electricity could transform manufacturing competitiveness, demand for consumer durables and the rural non-farm economy.

Private entry into distribution cannot be sustained unless organised theft is eliminated and T&D losses brought down to levels considered normal across the World. This requires taking on the T&D mafia that diverts half of available electricity into the black market for personal gain. The arguments about whether rich or poor steal more electricity are a red herring. The T&D mafia is deeply entrenched in the State Electricity Boards and their successor distribution companies and ensures that political patrons share in the loot so that nobody questions or exposes them. The mafia can only be controlled by a combination of peoples power (Resident Welfare Associations), sustained reporting by media, legal changes (power to acquire the ill gotten assets of SEB/ distribution company employees) and administrative/police action. Success requires recognition by all protagonists that a T&D mafia is being confronted, not individuals stealing power.

During the debate on the Electricity Bill (2003) the opposition rightly wanted more independent and stronger regulators. It agreed to facilitate passage of the Bill only after the govt. promised to bring in the desired amendments at a subsequent date. Since the opposition became the govt. an ill fated attempt to weaken (rather than strengthen) the regulator has thankfully been thwarted. The delay in implementation has, however, increased regulatory risk, whereas professional, secure regulators would reduce it. The noises from several State governments similarly suggest a desire to weaken rather than enhance open access by non-transparent and dilatory setting of access charges. Pricing of access is a regulatory function and regulators must be empowered with the authority and the professional capability to discharge this function, if policy and regulatory risk is to be eliminated.

12.3.9. FDI

The fourth reform that can structurally transform the economy is the integration of Indian manufacturing in the Global supply chain. This involves both policy and institutional reforms. The second half of the 20th century has been characterised by a fragmentation of production and outsourcing of many stages of the manufacturing process. Though it started with domestic outsourcing, it has crossed the border during the last quarter of the century, so that an increasing amount of World trade is intra-industry trade in intermediate goods.

12.3.10. Bureaucratic Mindset

Most important is a change in the mindset of the Indian bureaucracy in its attitude to private investment and production, both domestic and foreign. Institutional reform that makes the bureaucracy responsible for aggregate production, employment and investment could accelerate TFPG and capital deepening. The labour and education policies suggested above would not only help the pace of global integration but also multiply the benefits to labour.

12.3.11. Government

The government's thirst for intervention in all spheres of economic and social activity has far exceeded its ability to achieve positive outcomes in any of them. The high moral fervour that characterised the political leaders and the positive motivations that drove the administration at the time of independence has long since faded. There is a large gap between the theory of Government intervention and the Practice of governance in a low-income democratic country. In theory market failure has been used to justify the production of all kinds of goods and services by the government. In practice the problem of government failure is now much more serious. In theory ownership of the means of production by the government should result in efficiency equal to private ownership and greater equity. In practice government production and supply is characterised by lower efficiency and either no gains in equity or the creation of new inequity. The high moral purpose assumed to be present in public functionaries does not exist and incentives systems for motivating desired behaviour (e.g. profit maximisation or cost minimisation) cannot be sustained in the public sector because of political over lord ship.

The theoretical accountability of politicians to voters is thwarted in practice by sharing misappropriated public resources with special interest groups whose vote is critical to re-election. All interventions are justified by the ministers and administrations as in the public interest or in the name of the poor or both. This professed concern of government for the public, contrasts sharply with the neglect of public goods & services that are the traditional & accepted responsibilities of every government. One such responsibility is the security of life and property (policing).

12.4. Conclusion

Historically, economic development and growth have been characterised by a shift of labour from low productive agriculture to high productive manufacturing leading to acceleration in factor productivity (TFPG). In this process labour first migrates from rural areas traditional urban services before moving on to urban industrial jobs. Our highly rigid labour policy for the organised sector, along with SSI reservation, has thwarted this transition from traditional agriculture to modern industry. Given the difficulty of reducing labour supply even when there is no demand for products modern industry has the incentive minimise use of labour. It has done so by adopting more capital and skill intensive techniques to minimise market demand risk and by fragmenting into smaller units to escape these laws. Though industry can and will continue to grow, it will not generate employment at the rate that it could have, unless labour laws are made more flexible and employment oriented.

An additional factor in the structural transformation is universal primary education. Such education teaches not just reading and writing but the new type of discipline of working with machines that have their own rhythm and requirement (different from nature dependent agriculture). Government has a vital role in ensuring universal primary education. Given the lack of accountability and high cost of supply of government education, the non-profit sector can play an important role even the supply of schooling if the right policy framework and regulatory system is put in place. The non-govt. sector (non-profit and commercial), constrained so far by the constitution and courts, can play an equally vital role in promoting technical, higher and professional education.

Compulsory rating of education providers and standardised disclosure of accounts and fees can help solve much of the problem and allow removal of conventional, oppressive, bureaucratic controls and approvals. Electricity is the most important intermediate input into modern industry no matter how labour intensive. Its ready availability could have transformed rural areas into semi urban hubs of industrial activity (given road and telecom connectivity) that could thrive as genuine small-scale industry (rather than the hot house variety nurtured by excise exemptions).

Modern competitive markets are essential for modern industry to grow and flourish and these cannot exist without the Rule of Law and public security. Producers must be physically connected (permanent roads) to each other and to consumers. Both connectivity and security of people and goods are essential for the division of labour to take place in a sustained and effective manner. The government has over the years since independence, spread itself so widely and thinly over so many problems and issues that it is unable to supply these public goods that are its primary responsibility.

The scenario of employment in 2020 will develop based on certain underlying trends in regard to factors, which prevail in the longer term. Though the growth of labour force will slow down, but the elasticity of employment will also fall, which means that pressure on labour market will not ease. As agricultural work opportunities continue to shrink, the informal sector will grow rapidly. To cope up with such expected trends, strategies are needed to promote labour intensive and capital saving technologies. Employment creation in small establishments will have to be promoted by incentives linked with jobs created rather than capital invested. Migrant labour will increase social pressures. A strategy to raise the wage levels of those who migrate will have to be based on a massive programme for development of vocational skills. A simple but broad based social security system will have to be developed to improve quality of employment in a scenario where migrant workers will be rapidly growing. Such a social security system coupled with better labour incomes, based on better productivity of trained manpower, will facilitate the conversion of emerging work opportunities into meaningful jobs, where chances of extreme exploitation of labour get eliminated.

References

Gupta, S.P., "Targeting Ten Million Employment Opportunities a Year in the Tenth Plan period", *Report of Special Group*, Planning Commission, Government of India, 2002.

Government of India, *Ninth Five Year Plan*, Planning Commission, 1999.

Government of India, Task Force on "Employment Opportunities", Planning Commission, 2001.

13

Demographic Security

13.1. Introduction

Recognition of the demographic transition as a security-relevant process could inspire researchers to delve deeper into relationships between demographic factors and armed conflict and encourage policymakers to become familiar with the foreign policies and international programmes that have influenced the speed of demographic transition. As a stabilising process in nation-states, progress along the demographic transition receives much less recognition and research focus from most quarters of the security community than promotion of democracy and market reforms. This may be an error. In recent years some analysts have argued that, in the absence of major social changes, pushing democratisation and economic liberalisation can inspire civil unrest.

In the early 1970s, women in almost every developing country were estimated to have, on average, more than four children during their lives. In the three decades that followed, a revolution in child-bearing spread across the world. Yet progress along the demographic transition has been uneven and lags in several regions. Patterns of modern decline in fertility correspond closely to increased use of modern contraception. And the results of national and local studies suggest that declines in both fertility and childhood mortality have reinforced each other. In certain regions of the world, however, most countries have made far less progress along the demographic transition. More than one-third of all countries remain in the transition's early and middle phases. That is, rates of birth and death-particularly the deaths of infants, children and women in pregnancy and childbirth-remain high in most of sub-Saharan Africa and in parts of South and Central Asia.

And birth rates remain high despite relatively low death rates in much of the Middle East and in several Latin American countries and Pacific Islands.

A new, demographically significant force has emerged in the last 25 years, unforeseen by those who first developed the model of the demographic transition. Death rates have actually reversed their decline in more than 30 countries, most in sub-Saharan Africa, due largely to the HIV/aids pandemic. In some formerly communist Eastern European countries, rising death rates involve other aspects of declining public health, such as increasing alcoholism and tobacco use, a tuberculosis epidemic, environmental health problems, and a rollback in the quality of affordable health services. In a few countries-notably Rwanda and East Timor-recent civil conflicts themselves boosted death rates significantly. By themselves, annual rates of birth and death seem like the driest and most basic of all national statistics.

In general, the longer a girl remains in school, the fewer births she is likely to have. Some of the regional variation in this relationship is probably due to the differences in women's economic opportunities provided by attaining higher levels of education, and differences in the trade-offs (what economists call opportunity costs) in terms of child-bearing that are needed to realise those opportunities. Some variation may be produced by regional differences in the amount of control women have over decisions related to child-bearing, and regional differences in their access to affordable contraception.

Population growth or decline, domestic demand for food, fresh water and energy, urbanisation (increasing proportions of a population in and around cities), and international migration all fall under the sway of birth and death rates. Trends in birth, death and migration determine a population's age structure (the proportions of people in each age group relative to the population as a whole), which in turn determines the ratio of dependents to economically active people, the relative size of the school-age population, and the numbers of those entering and leaving the workforce. Clearly, any one of these forces can exert a vast array of political, social, economic, and environmental influences upon society.

13.2. Outbreaks of Civil Conflict and Demographic Transition

The likelihood of experiencing an outbreak of civil conflict in the 1990s was highest for countries in the early and middle phases of demographic transition. Each point represents a country, in terms of its birth and death rate, 1985-1990. The curved line traces the general path of countries as they proceeded along the demographic transition during the late 1980s, at the close of the Cold War. During the next decade, most countries in civil conflict were situated left of the curve's trough. Few countries to the right, in the vicinity of population equilibrium (diagonal dotted line), experienced an outbreak of civil conflict.

Decline in the likelihood of civil conflict mirrored progress along the demographic transition, from the 1970s through the 1990s. During the 1970s and '80s, however, only a handful of developing countries had made substantial progress through the demographic transition, and Eastern and Southern European countries had not yet reached the low rates of birth (annual births per 1,000 people) currently experienced.

13.2.1. Process of Demographic Transition

All countries are going through this process or have passed through it. Individually, birthrate and deathrate transitions have taken from 50 to 150 years to complete. Some developing countries are passing through these transitions very rapidly, much faster than European or North American countries did. Population growth and decline are results of gaps between birth rates and death rates (measured per thousand people). Because death rates typically decrease before birth rates begin to decline, population tends to grow rapidly during the transition.

The infant mortality rates in the table are the average of this measure in the countries falling in the birth rate categories listed to their left. There is speculation, however, that the demographic transition's effects on age structure and workforce growth are improving the chances of success for peace negotiations occurring in Northern Ireland and Sri Lanka. The demographic transition's influence on the world's states, as a group, has been both impressive and sustained. Risk was highest among countries that entered the 1990s with very high birth rates (greater than or equal to 45 births per thousand people) and relatively high infant mortality rates. Nearly half of the countries in this category experienced a new conflict. And declines in birth rates and infant mortality rates corresponded closely to declines in the risk of armed conflict. A decline in the birth rate of five births per thousand people corresponded to a decline of just over 5 per cent in the risk of civil conflict. A further analysis of the 1970s and 1980s shows that there were similar transition-related effects during those Cold War decades.

A better understanding of the demographic transition suggests what the answer might be. Although the transition is a continuous process, it may be best understood as a succession of five phases. All of today's countries have already emerged from the first of these-the pre-transition phase, which dominated most of human history. In this phase women fortunate enough to survive their reproductive years typically experienced many live births, but half or more of these children died before age five. Because global human population grew very slowly until a few centuries ago, demographers assume that few populations living before the modern era ever moved beyond the pre-transition phase. This assumption is supported by historical, archeological and anthropological research indicating that infant and maternal mortality tended to be much higher, and average adult lifespan much shorter than today.

Today, all countries belong in one of the next four phases: the early-transition, middle-transition, late-transition, and post-transition phases. A population's progress through these phases is most easily understood in terms of two components: birth rates and death rates. The adjoining maps, however, are colour-coded using a single, more straightforward measure: a country's total fertility rate, which is an estimate of the average number of live births per woman during her lifetime, and a reasonable gauge of the average family size. Of particular interest to analysts who track recent population dynamics are the countries near replacement fertility-the level of slightly more than two children per woman at which populations would ultimately level off and stop growing in the absence of migration, assuming low mortality rates throughout the childhood and the reproductive years.

13.2.1.1. Transition from Turmoil

Progress in nutrition, sanitation, and prevention and treatment of infectious disease have historically brought populations into a second stage of the demographic transition-the early-transition phase, during which childhood death rates decline while birth rates remain high. Birth rates have tended to decrease less readily than death rates not only because of cultural preferences for many children and long lives, but also because techniques for preventing unwanted pregnancy have tended to be more complicated, less diverse and much more controversial than those available for extending life. The gap that develops between birth and death rates in this early stage of transition produces several important demographic features. Perhaps the most notable is rapid population growth, but other outcomes are unusually large proportions of children and adolescent dependents and a relative dearth of working age adults per dependent.

In recent decades, this phase has coincided with an upsurge in the use of modern contraception, and often has been characterised by elongated delays before marriage and before girls end schooling, and falling rates of pregnancy-related deaths. Declines in fertility begin to advance the population's median age (the age at which the number of those older is exactly equal to those younger). Unless substantial migration intervenes, the population growth rate slows. However, birth rates typically remain far above death rates and population continues to climb. Further population growth and maturation of the age structure continue in the late-transition phase. As fertility approaches the two-child-per-woman level, youth become a smaller proportion of the population than in earlier phases, and the elderly begin to comprise a larger proportion. Death rates rise, reflecting a slow increase in the diseases of old age, away from the high incidence of childhood illnesses common in earlier phases. Until late-transition populations acquire a more mature age structure, death rates tend to remain lower than birth rates. This phenomenon, which demographers call population momentum, can extend population growth for four to six decades after replacement fertility is reached. And this momentum is currently the major source of population growth in numerous countries that, within the last several decades, attained fertility levels near replacement or below-including China (total fertility rate of 1.8 children per woman, in 2000-05), Iran (2.3 children per woman), Tunisia (2.0), Indonesia (2.3), Vietnam (2.3), Thailand (1.9), and Brazil (2.2).

The demographic future is unclear for countries in the post-transition phase, where the momentum of population growth has run its course. One post-transitional characteristic is a near certainty: that the population's elderly proportion will grow larger than ever before-commonly to around one-fifth of the whole, according to UN projections. In some cases this proportion could become higher than one-third, at least temporarily. Population decline is a possibility throughout the industrial world, and a current reality in more than a dozen countries, including Russia, Italy and much of Eastern Europe. Due to decades of below-replacement-level fertility, the age structures of some European countries are likely to lead (in the absence of major increases in migration) to population decline over the next several decades-a phenomenon demographers call negative population momentum.

13.2.1.2. Transition's opportunities

Where the demographic transition is in its latter phases, societies face opportunities and challenges attributable to the transition's effects on age structure. As fertility nears the replacement level, small families become common and working-age adults assume a large proportion of the population. These trends encourage household savings, lessen the burdens on public schools and other government services, increase the number of taxable adults per dependent, and help families invest more in each child. Some economists refer to this one-time bulge in the workforce and simultaneous rise in the support ratio-the number of working-age adults per child-as a demographic bonus.

13.2.2. Stages of Demographic Transition

The populations of countries, such as Afghanistan, that are in the early phase of the demographic transition typically have age structures that exhibit a predominance of young adults (commonly called a youth bulge) and children. As countries advance into the late phase of transition-shown by the population age structure of South Korea-the proportion of children begins to drop off, but a youth bulge persists for a decade or two, moving "upward" into the older age classes. France's population has a more mature age structure, typical of populations that have passed through the demographic transition into the post-transition phase.

13.2.2.1. Post-transition population

In the 1960s and early 1970s, states in East and Southeast Asia (including South Korea, Thailand, Taiwan, Malaysia and Indonesia) expanded access to public education and primary health and family planning services. Fertility declined rapidly over the ensuing decades. People lived longer, married later in life and, with smaller families, saved a relatively large portion of their wages and spent more on educating each child. When labour force growth began to slow in the late 1980s, wages rose. Attracted by the pay, women entered the manufacturing workforce in large numbers. Then fertility declined again. As their labour forces grew increasingly educated and urbanised, these states-which economists dubbed the Asian Tigers-adjusted their business and trade policies to encourage investments from technologically advanced manufacturing industries in North America and Japan. Endowed with unusually high savings rates, the Asian Tigers actually exported financial capital to the West until they were hit by a regional economic downdraft in the late 1990s. Today other developing countries that have recently attained late-transition status-including Sri Lanka, Mexico, China, Iran, Tunisia and Vietnam-have evolved age structures that are favourable to economic growth. And this development could help ease civil tensions where they exist.

13.2.2.2. Transition's challenges

Some economists and demographers are alarmed by the prospect of deleterious effects on social cohesion and economic prosperity from a post-transitional aging population and decline in the size of the workforce. This is uncertain terrain. Industrial countries are just beginning to grapple with the challenges of a shrinking workforce and a large and growing proportion of the elderly. So far, none have shown overt signs of unusual economic or political instability because of it-including Russia, where the median age has risen to 38 years and population is declining by around 1 million people (0.7 per cent) annually. Inevitably, all states must face some degree of demographic challenge as they approach population stability or experience population decline. And, in contrast to the minimal capacity of many developing countries to adjust to continuing rapid population growth, industrial countries have considerable capacity to adjust to aging and decline in population.

Some adjustment is already occurring. Confronted with a growing proportion of elderly, some European states have worked to maintain lower ratios of workers to retirees by accepting more immigrants, extending the retirement age, and attracting more women into the workforce while making it easier for them to raise children while working. Japan, while reluctant to accept a large number of immigrants, is experimenting with several of these options, as well as returning some of the responsibility for elder care to families. To deal with a shrinking workforce, Japan is continuing to replace low-skill jobs with technology and to move its less innovative, labour-intense industries overseas. The Japanese government has committed to worker re-training programmes and stepped up investments in research and development.

13.2.2.3. Asian Tiger Model of Development

In several East and Southeast Asian countries, including South Korea and Thailand, declines in fertility largely preceded the period of rapid economic growth. In these countries, which economists refer to as the Asian Tigers, fertility decline may have helped prepare societies for economic change and democratisation. Fertility is estimated by the total fertility rate, and income per person is estimated by gross national income per capita. Downturns in average income between 1995 and 2000 are associated with the Asian currency crisis that began in 1996.

13.2.2.4. Demographic Dimensions of Conflict

Tensions run especially high when such a demographic shift is led by an ethnic population-often a group in a high-growth stage of the demographic transition-that threatens to challenge numerically a politically powerful group. These changes are difficult to quantify, as detailed ethnic data are unavailable from most countries (some, like Lebanon, suppress collection of these data to lessen tensions). Ethnic suspicions and fears often have been cultivated as a foundation for political organisation and, on occasion, worked up into hatred and political violence. Refugee movements and other cross-border migrations regularly evoke fears and anti-immigrant tensions in host countries.

Rapid, composition-altering migrations of politically powerful groups may represent the most direct demographic contributions to interethnic tensions. Throughout history, such migrations have foreshadowed the alteration or elimination of local institutions, cultural traditions and patterns of land use and control, producing some of today's most volatile fault lines of ethnic confrontation. Among the examples of this are Han settlements in western China, European and mestizo farmers abutting native communities throughout the Americas, Israeli settlements on the West Bank, Javanese on Indonesia's outer islands, and North Indians and Bengalis in the Tibeto-Burmese-speaking regions of eastern India. Slower, more predictable shifts in ethnic composition also can play an influential role in the emergence of political tensions. Current demographic trends in Lebanon, Israel, Estonia and Fiji indicate future changes in ethnic or religious composition that, if continued, could precipitate constitutional crises or even civil violence. And for larger countries with populous and growing regional ethnicities, the rise of ethnic separatism remains a perpetual possibility.

Despite a consensus that the relative sizes and distributions of ethnic populations in a country are important, political scientists are deeply divided as to what measures of ethnic populations reflect risks of state failure or civil conflict. And because this theoretical uncertainty is exacerbated by a lack of data, differential population growth among ethnic and religious groups, and flows of refugees and other migrants were not included in our analyses. In a world that, in the last 50 years, has experienced unprecedented population growth, a four-fold growth in independent states and vastly uneven economic growth between them-and where the vast majority of national boundaries were drawn by conquerors and colonial administrators rather than through democratic processes-immigration and ethnic population shifts are bound to remain sources of political stress. And policies and trends that influence migration, ethnic relations, separatism and assimilation warrant intense study and the collection of more accurate data.

13.3. End of the Transition

Since the early 1960s, fertility in the world's developing countries has declined on average by half, and infant mortality by two-thirds. Population growth rates in these countries are down by more than half. These trends are currently among the most hopeful of all that influence social and economic development and political stability in some of the poorest countries. The lion's share of the credit for this transformation goes to those developing countries that have invested in improving access to family planning, maternal and child health care and other reproductive health services, and have followed through on policies that brought more girls into classrooms and more women into workplaces. These policies bolstered women's status and income, indirectly improved child nutrition, increased child survival, and expanded demand for modern contraception. The states of the industrialised world can share credit in these achievements. A handful of donor countries, including the United States, the Scandinavian countries, the Netherlands and Japan, have provided critical financing, training, expertise and leadership, either through their own programmes or through the United Nations Population Fund.

Support for international family planning efforts has waned, however, in recent years-and at an inopportune time. The need for more and better quality reproductive health care, contraceptives and counselling is growing. Nearly 1.1 billion young people aged 15 to 19 are entering their reproductive years, most of them unaware of the risks and responsibilities of sex and reproduction. Three million people die each year from aids. And still, around 515,000 women perish annually from largely preventable pregnancy-related causes, including about 70,000 deaths from unsafe abortions.

Growth of global population is decelerating more dramatically than was anticipated even in the mid-1990s. The United Nations Population Division, the most widely consulted demographic accountant on these matters, has set its 2002 medium variant projection-the one the division deems most predictive-at 7.9 billion people in 2025. That's about 1.5 billion more people than today. But it is also nearly 600 million fewer than the same UN demographers had projected for 2025 just a decade earlier. Yet, the growth rate of population would be slower still if not for the fact that an estimated 38 per cent of all pregnancies worldwide-some 80 million annually-are either unintended at the time or unwanted at any time.

The global demographic transition is still far from complete. While one-third of the world's countries have made their way fully through the transition, more than a third remains in the early and middle phases. The future could see a continuation of today's impressive declines in fertility and childhood mortality, and a reversal in the HIV/AIDS pandemic-but only if policymakers support and fund the policies and programmes that make such change possible. If the relationships between the demographic transition and conflict seen in the post-Cold War years hold in the coming decades, decisions made today that affect funding that facilitates this momentous transition could have an enormous influence, not only on demographic prospects, but also on the future of global security.

Demographic transition is the transformation of a population from conditions of short life expectancy and large families to long life expectancy and small families. About one third of the world's countries-those with the longest histories of access to life-saving technologies and effective contraception-are in the last stage of this transition. At least another third of the world's countries, however, are still in the early and middle phases of the transition, in which death rates are low compared to historic levels, but birth rates remain relatively high. Such countries typically experience large proportions of young people and rapid population growth.

Population age structure has important implications. Some developing countries in the middle and late phases of the demographic transition experience a window of opportunity to exploit a demographic bonus-a large working-age population relative to proportionally smaller populations of dependent children and older people. The post-transition phase that many industrialised countries have entered typically leads to population aging and eventual population decline, absent offsetting migration. Such conditions are likely to challenge retirement systems and labour markets, but the influences of population aging on the civil and political order remain speculative and arguably helps dampen the likelihood of conflict.

In recent decades the world as a whole has moved fairly rapidly through the early and middle stages of the demographic transition. Average family size is now a bit more than half of what it was in the early 1960s, and infant mortality has declined by two thirds. Policies and investments that improved family planning and related reproductive health services and brought more girls into the classroom and women into the workplace are major reasons for this progress. Waning international support for family planning services, however, renders uncertain the pace of further progress through the transition.

References

Birdsall N, Kelley A.C, Sinding S.W (eds)., *Population Matters: Demographic Change, Economic Growth and Poverty in the Developing World,* London: Oxford Univ. Press, 2001

Livi-Bacci M., *A Concise History of World Population,* Cambridge, MA: Blackwell, 1992.

Lutz W, Goujon A., "The World's Changing Human Capital Stock: Multi-state Population Forecasts by Educational Attainment", *Population and Development Review,* 2001.

Mansfield, E.D, Snyder J., "Democratization and the Danger of War", *International Security,* 1995

Marshall MG, Khosla D., *Peace and Conflict 2001: A Global Survey of Armed Conflicts, Self-Determination Movements, and Democracy,* College Park: Center for International Development and Conflict Management, University of Maryland, 2001.

Nichiporuk B., "The Security Dynamics of Demographic Factors," Santa Monica: RAND, 2000

Zakaria F., *The Future of Freedom,* New York: W.W. Norton, 2003

Bibliography

Ashford, Lori S., "New Population Policies: Advancing Women's Health and Rights," *Population Bulletin* 56, no. 1, 2001.

Baubock, R., Heller, A. & Zolberg,A. (Eds)., "The challenge of diversity: Integration andpluralism in societies of immigration", 1996.

Beaver, S. E., *Demographic Transition Theory Reinterpreted,* Lexington, MA: Lexington Books, 1975.

Berry, J.W., "Immigration, acculturation and adaptation", *Applied Psychology,* 1997.

_______________ ., J.S. Phinney, D.L. Sam & P. Vedder (Eds.), "Immigrant youth in culturaltransition: Acculturation, identity and adaptation across national context", Mahwah, NJ:Lawrence Erlbaum Associates, 2006.

Birdsall N, Kelley A.C, Sinding S.W (eds)., *Population Matters: Demographic Change, Economic Growth and Poverty in the Developing World,* London: Oxford Univ. Press, 2001

Bloom, D and Williamson, J., "Demographic transitions and economic miracles in emerging Asia", *World Bank Economic Review,* 1998.

_______________ , "Global demographic change: dimensions and economic significance, In Global demographic change: economic impacts and policy challenges", *proceedings of a symposium,* sponsored by the Federal Reserve Bank of Kansas City Jackson Hole, Wyoming - August 26-28, 2004.

_______________ , Canning, D and Sevilla, J., "The demographic dividend: a new perspective on the economic consequences of population change", *RAND Population Matters Monograph Series,* Santa Monica, California: RAND Corporation, 2003.

Bold, "Health Status of Elderly in India" *International Institute of Ageing,* United Nations, Malta, 2001

Bose, A, "Fighting Female Foeticide - Growing Greed and Shrinking Child Sex Ratio", *Economic and Political Weekly,* 8 Sep., 2001.

Buckwalter, Donald W. and Dean S. Rugg, "Delimiting the Physical City: Disparities Between Various Methods of Calculating Population Density," *Professional Geographer*, 1986,

Carter Brandon and Kirsten Honmann, "Valuing Environmental Costs in India: The Economy Wide Impact of Environment Degradation", World Bank, mimeo, 1991-92.

Chesnais, J. C., *The Demographic Transition: Stages, Patterns and Economic Implications,* trans. E. Kreager and P. Kreager. Oxford, UK: Clarendon Press, 1992.

Chowdhry, P., "Crisis of Masculinity in Haryana The Unmarried, the Unemployed and the Aged", *Economic and Political Weekly*, 2005.

Coale, A.J and Hoover, E.M., "Population growth and economic development in low-income countries", Princeton NJ: Princeton University Press, 1958.

Crawford, J., W. Acevedo, T. Foresman, J. Buchanan, and W. Prince, "Developing a Temporal Database of Urban Development for the Baltimore/Washington Region," *paper presented at the American Society for Photogrammetry and Remote Sensing annual conference*, Baltimore, MD, 1996.

Dasgupta, J., "National Population Policy 2000: A Critique", *Seminar on the New Paradigm of Development and Sex Selection,* New Delhi, India, 2004.

Dyson, Tim, "India's Population: The Past," in *Twenty-First Century India: Population, Economy, Human Development, and the Environment*, ed., Tim Dyson, Robert Cassen, and Leela Visaria, New York: Oxford University Press, 2004.

________________, Robert Cassen, and Leela Visaria, eds., *Twenty-First Century India: Population, Economy, Human Development, and the Environment,* New York: Oxford University Press, 2004.

Ehrlich, P., *The population bomb*, USA: Sierra Club Books, 1968.

ESCAP, *Population of India, Country Monograph Series* no. 10, New York: United Nations, 1982.

Foresman, TimothyW., Steward T.A. Pickett, and Wayne C. Zipperer, "Methods for Spatial and Temporal Land Use and Land Cover Assessment for Urban Ecosystems and Application in the Greater Baltimore-Chesapeake Region," *Urban Ecosystems*, 1997.

George, S. M., "Sex selection/determination in India : contemporary developments", *Reproductive Health Matters*, Vol. 10, 2002.

Goldstein, Sidney, "Urbanization in China, 1982-87: Effects of Migration and Reclassification," *Population and Development Review*, 1990.

Government of India, *Ninth Five Year Plan*, Planning Commission, 1999.

Government of India, Task Force on "Employment Opportunities", Planning Commission, 2001.

Green, C.P., "The Environment and Population Growth: Decade for Action", *Population Reports*, Series M, No. 10, Vol. XX, No. 2, Baltimore, Johns Hopkins School of Public Health, Population Information Program, 1992.

Gulati, S. C., "Population-Development-Environmental Linkages in India", *Paper presented in Millennim Conference on Population*, Development and Environment Nexus organised by IASP, PFI and UNFPA at New Delhi, February 14-16, 2000.

Gupta, I., P. Dasgupta and M. Sawhney, " Health of the Elderly in India: Some Aspects of Vulnerability" *Discussion paper series No 26*, Institute of Economic Growth, University Enclave, Delhi-7, 2001.

Gupta, S.P., "Targeting Ten Million Employment Opportunities a Year in the Tenth Plan period", *Report of Special Group*, Planning Commission, Government of India, 2002.

Jha, P., Kumar,R., Vasa P., et al, "Low male-to-female sex ratio of children born in India: national survey of 1.1 million households", The Lancet (online) available at www.thelancet.com, 2006.

John Bongaarts, "The Fertility-Inhibiting Effects of the Intermediate Fertility Variables", *Studies in Family Planning*, Vol. 13, No. 6/7. Jun. - Jul., 1982.

Johnston, Denis F. and Michael J. Carley, "Social Measurement and Social Indicators", *Annals of the American Academy of Political and Social Science*, 1981.

Kingdon, Greta et al., "Education and Literacy," in *Twenty-First Century India: Population, Economy, Human Development, and the Environment*, ed. Tim Dyson, Robert Cassen, and Leela Visaria, New York: Oxford University Press, 2004.

Kutta, Fratisek, Michal Illner, "System of Social Indicators and Elaboration of the Information Basis for Social Planning and Forecasting", *Sociologicky-Casopis*, 1983.

Kuznets, S., "Population and economic growth", in *Proceedings of the American Philosophical Society*, III (3), 1967.

Land, Kenneth C., "Social Indicators", *Annual Review of Sociology*, Vol. 9: 1-26, 1983.

Larsen, M and Hatti, N., "Family Structures and Declining Child Sex Ratios in India", *Part of a series within ongoing project Lives at*

Risk: Discrimination of Female Children in modern India, Swedish Research Council, Preliminary paper, 2004.

Livi-Bacci M., *A Concise History of World Population,* Cambridge, MA: Blackwell, 1992.

Livi-Bici, M., *The Population of Europe,* trans. C. De Nardi Ispen and C. Ispen. Malden, MA: Blackwell, 1999.

Longman, Phillip, *The Empty Cradle: how falling birth rates threaten global prosperity and what to do about it,* 2004.

Lutz W, Goujon A., "The World's Changing Human Capital Stock: Multi-state Population Forecasts by Educational Attainment", *Population and Development Review,* 2001.

Ma, Lawrence J. C. And Chusheng Li, "Development of Towns in China: A Case Study of Guangdong Province," Population and Development Review, 1993.

Mangahas, Mahar, "Measurement of Poverty and Equity: Some ASEAN Social Indicators Experience", *Social Indicators Research,* 1983.

Mansfield, E.D, Snyder J., "Democratization and the Danger of War", *International Security,* 1995

Marshall MG, Khosla D., *Peace and Conflict 2001: A Global Survey of Armed Conflicts, Self-Determination Movements, and Democracy,* College Park: Center for International Development and Conflict Management, University of Maryland, 2001.

McFalls, Joe, *Population: A Lively Introduction,* Population Reference Bureau, 2007

McIntyre, N.E., K. Knowles-Yanez, and D. Hope, "Urban Ecology as an Interdisciplinary Field: Differences in the Use of 'Urban' Between the, Social and Natural Sciences," *Urban Ecosystems,* 2000.

Natarajan, K.S., *Population Growth in 21st century, Paper presented in the meeting of the Group on Vision 2020.*

Nichiporuk B., "The Security Dynamics of Demographic Factors," Santa Monica: RAND, 2000

Patel, V., "Adverse Juvenile sex ratio in Kerala", *Economic and Political Weekly,* June, 2002.

Preston, Samuel, Patrick Heuveline, and Michel Guillot, *Demography: Measuring and Modeling Population Processes,* Blackwell Publishing, 2000.

Reddy, P. H., " The health of the aged in India", *Health Transition Review,* 1996.

Saksena, H. S., "Issues concerning vulnerable groups", *Paper presented in the meeting of the Group on Vision 2020.*

Shreeniwas, Sudha, "Family Size, Sex Composition and Children's Education: Ethnic Differentials over Development in Peninsular Malaysia," *Population Studies,* Vol. 51, No. 2, July 1997.

Singh, Padam, "Trends in Fertility, mortality, nutrition and Health indicator", *Paper presented in the meeting of the Group on Vision 2020.*

South, S. J., Trent, K., "Sex Ratios and Women's Roles: A Cross-National Analysis", *American Journal of Sociology,* Vol. 93, Issue 5, March 1988.

Srininvasn, K., "Population projections of India and the larger states based on 2001 census results", Paper presented *in the meeting of the Group on Vision 2020.*

Swami Agnivesh, "Child Labour", Paper presented *in the meeting of the Group on Vision 2020.*

UNFPA, "Sex Selective Abortions and Fertility Decline: The Case of Haryana and Punjab", New Delhi, India, 2001.

UNICEF Media Centre, "UNICEF endorses multi-faith campaign against female foeticide", Available at: http://www.unicef.org/india/media_1030.html, 2005.

Unisa, S., Prakasam, C.P., Sinha,R.K Bhagat, R.B., "Evidence of Sex Selective Abortion from Two Cultural Settings of India: A Study of Haryana and Tamil Nadu" International Institute for Population Sciences, Mumbai, India, 2003.

United Nations Population Division, *World Immigration Report,* New York, 2002.

_______________ , *World population prospects,* the 2004 revision, United Nations, New York, February, 2005.

United Nations, "World Population 2000", *United Nations,* Population Division, Department of Economic and Social Affairs, New York, 2001.

Varghese, J. Aruldas, V., & Jeemon P., "Analysis of Trends in Sex Ratio at Birth of Hospitalized Deliveries in the State of Delhi", Christian Medical Association of India, July, New Delhi, India, 2005.

Visaria and Visaria, "India's Population in Transition"; and International Institute for Population Sciences (IIPS), *Reproductive and Child Health: District Level Household Survey 2002-04,* Mumbai: Government of India, 2006.

Visaria, Leela and Pravin Visaria, "India's Population in Transition," *Population Bulletin*, 40, no. 3, 1995.

Wattenberg, Ben J., *How the New Demography of Depopulation Will Shape Our Future*, Chicago: R. Dee, 2004.

WHO, "Our Planet, Our Earth", *Report of the WHO Commission on Health and Environment*, World Health Organization, Geneva, 1992.

Zakaria F., *The Future of Freedom*, New York: W.W. Norton, 2003

Index